Contents

Education

Unit 1	Schools	1
Unit 2	School issues	15
Unit 3	Higher education	28

The world

Unit 4	Money makes the world go round!	43
Unit 5	Our political world	56
Unit 6	World poverty	69

The natural world

Unit 7	The weather	82
Unit 8	Today's world adventurers	95
Unit 9	Problem Earth	107

The arts

Unit 10	Dance and movement	120
Unit 11	Cinema	132
Unit 12	Every picture tells a story	145

History

Unit 13 Life then and now   158

Unit 14 Medicine through the ages   171

Unit 15 Up, up and away!   184

Science and technology

Unit 16 The appliance of science   196

Unit 17 Science, technology and the body   211

Unit 18 The Big Bang   224

The accompanying CD contains a listening exercise for each unit in this Coursebook. There are 18 tracks on the CD and the track number corresponds to the unit number, for example CD Track 1 is for Unit 1, Schools.

Unit 1 Schools

A Let's start

1 Think about and answer these questions with a friend.
- When did you start back at school?
- What were the first days like?
- Did anything or anyone surprise you? What? Who?

My first week at school

Monday	Thursday
Tuesday	Friday
Wednesday	Saturday	Sunday

Now look at the diary on the left and copy and complete it with the things that happened during your first week. You can include names of new friends or your teachers' names; things you did that you liked or disliked; and things you did that are the same as or different from the year before.

2 Compare your diary with your friend's. How are they the same or different? Talk about the information that you have put in your diaries.

3 This is language you learnt in Coursebook 1. Can you remember what each person is saying?

4 With your friend, copy and complete the table below with information about your school. Ask your teacher if there are any words that you don't know how to spell or don't know in English.

Question	Answer
1 Do you have one classroom or do you go to different classrooms for different subjects?	
2 What new subjects are you learning this year?	
3 What are the names of your teachers and what subjects are they teaching you?	
4 What is the name of your school's head teacher?	
5 How many pupils are there in your class?	
6 How many pupils are there in your school?	
7 Where do you keep your school books?	
8 What do you do about breakfast and lunch on a school day?	
9 How do most people in your class travel to and from school?	
10 Is your school large or small?	
11 Is your school urban or rural?	
12 Are boys and girls in the same class?	
13 How are the desks arranged in your classroom?	
14 When you want to address a teacher, how do you do it?	
15 Do you wear school uniform? If 'yes', describe it. If 'no', talk about what you wear.	
16 What facilities has your school got (e.g. computers, gym, swimming pool, etc.)?	
17 How long is your school day?	
18 Is your school private or public/state (government controlled)?	
19 How is your school similar to or different from other schools in your area?	
20 Does your school have a motto (slogan)? If 'yes', what is it? If 'no', what would you say are the aims of your school for its pupils?	
21 To what extent would you say the motto or the aims are achieved? Why/why not?	

B Let's read 1

1 You are going to read about public schools in Britain.

Note: In Britain, public schools can also be called private or independent schools, but they are fee-paying.

Before you read, look at the following features of public schools. Compare these with the school you go to and put a tick in the column which reflects your own school.

	✓	✗
The school day is long.	✓	
Scholarships are offered to attract brighter pupils.		
There is an emphasis on traditional academic subjects, such as maths, the classics, etc.		
Educational achievement is high.		
There is a small pupil–teacher ratio.		
The schools are free to select or reject any pupils they wish.		
The schools are competitive and academic.		
Some are either single-sex or denominational.		
Often there is a boarding school.		
There is a wide range of extra-curricular activities, e.g. youth and sports clubs.		
Pupils are encouraged to compete for the top universities in the country.		
The schools represent the wealthier members of society.		
Pupils who are highly motivated perform better.		
The standards of teaching are high.		
Exam results are high.		
Facilities are available for disabled pupils.		

- Can you think of any schools in your country that are similar to British public schools?
- What are the names of some of these schools in your country?
- What features would you say are the same and which are different?
- Would you like to go to a public school? Why/why not?

2 Read the extract below and find four points that match with the features on page 3. It is about twins who are starting at a new school called St Clare's. Their names are Pat and Isabel.

The twins soon found that St Clare's was quite different from their old school. Even the beds were not nearly so comfortable! And instead of being allowed to have their own pretty bedspreads and eiderdowns to match, every girl had to have the same.

"I hate being the same as everyone else!" said Pat. "Goodness — if only we were allowed to have what we liked, wouldn't we make everyone stare!"

"What I hate most is being one of the young ones," said Isabel dismally. "I hate being spoken to as if I were about six, when the top form or the fifth-form girls say anything to me. It's 'Here, you — get out of my way! Hi, you! Fetch me a book from the library!' It's too bad."

The standard of work was higher at St Clare's than at most schools, and although the twins had good brains, they found that they were rather behind their form in many ways, and this, too, annoyed them very much. They had so hoped that they would impress the others in so many ways — and it seemed as if they were even less than nobodies!

The twins were very much in awe of the older girls, who seemed very grown-up to them. The top form especially seemed almost as old and even more dignified than the mistresses. The head girl, Winifred James, spoke a few words to the twins the first week. She was a tall, clever-looking girl with pale blue eyes and pretty soft hair. St Clare's was proud of her; she had passed many difficult exams with flying colours.

One thing the twins found most annoying was the custom at St Clare's for the younger girls to wait on the two top forms. The fifth- and sixth-forms girls shared studies, two friends having a study between them.

They were allowed to furnish these studies themselves, very simply, and, in cold weather, to have their own fire there, and to have tea by themselves instead of in the hall with the others.

One day a girl came into the common room where the twins were reading and called to Janet (another pupil), "Hi, Janet — Kay Longden wants you. You're to light her fire and make some toast for her."

Janet got up without a word and went out. Pat and Isabel stared after her in surprise.

"Golly! What a cheek of Kay Longden to send a message to Janet like that! I'm jolly sure I wouldn't go and light anybody's fire!" said Pat.

"And neither would I," said Isabel. "Let one of the maids light it — or Kay herself."

3 Match the following words and expressions.

Golly!	Thick padded blankets
What a cheek	Tradition
Eiderdowns	With respect or wonder
Dismally	To do extremely well
In awe	Grand or majestic
Dignified	Unhappily or without interest
With flying colours	An expression of surprise
Custom	How rude

4 Decide whether the following are true or false in the text opposite.
   a) The school gave the twins their own bedding.
   b) The beds at the new school were comfortable.
   c) The twins thought they had nicer stuff than other girls
      in the school.
   d) The twins are six years old.
   e) The twins don't like the way the older girls talk to them.
   f) The twins were behind in lessons because they had
      good brains.
   g) The twins felt important at the school.
   h) The mistresses were the head girls.
   i) The school was proud of the head girl because she had
      done well at school.
   j) The two top forms were the fifth and sixth years.
   k) All the girls had their own studies.
   l) Janet seemed quite happy to do Kay's jobs.
   m) The twins thought a maid should do Kay's jobs.
   n) All the girls had to have their tea in the common room in
      the winter.

 C Let's speak and listen

1 You are going to hear six children talking about their school.
   Before you listen, look at the pictures on the next page and match
   the words/expressions in the box to each of the pictures. There are
   four words for each of the pictures.

   The 'Description number' will be filled in later, when you listen to
   the audio track.

denominational / Braille / violent / good facilities / outdoors / blind / disabled / lack of facilities / cultural centre / extra-curricular activities / sight-impaired / deaf / modern / segregated / sign language / lip-reading / unsafe / over-resourced / lack of pride and respect / poverty / hearing loss / lack of funding / extra tuition / graffiti

Words:	Words:	Words:
Description number:	Description number:	Description number:
Words:	Words:	Words:
Description number:	Description number:	Description number:

2 With your partner, talk about the different places illustrated above. Use the following points to help you:
- Where might you find each of the schools above?
- What sort of pupils would go to each of the schools?
- Do you know anybody who goes to any schools like those shown?
- What are the differences between each of the schools?

- Do you think boys and girls should/should not be separated for any of the schools above?
- How can schooling vary so much from place to place?
- Consider the reasons why schooling varies so much between different places.
- How could such schools help children in that society?
- What would society gain by sending children to such schools?

3 Now listen to the audio track, you will hear six pupils talking about their school. Match each of the descriptions to the pictures on page 6.

4 Listen again and write the words in Exercise 1 in the order that you hear them.

D Let's read 2

1 We have been looking at traditional or mainstream schools, which is what the majority of children attend. But there are schools that offer something different and are referred to as 'alternative schools'. In Coursebook 2 Unit 13 we learnt about Howard Gardner and his idea of multiple intelligences.

With your partner, talk about Howard Gardner and see what you can remember about him and his ideas.

The ideas of Howard Gardner are supported in alternative schools because it is felt that traditional schools don't respect the idea of multiple intelligences. Some people believe that the education system fails children because of this.

Alternative schools tend to favour freedom of choice rather than lessons or a timetable that everyone must follow. There can be more emphasis on outdoor activities or creativity than most mainstream schools allow. They tend to:
- have small classes
- be a smaller size overall
- give individual attention
- foster a sense of community.

2 With your partner you are going to talk about alternative schools and imagine that you could set one up. Talk about the following:

a) How would you make your alternative school different from the one you are at now?

b) What ideas would you introduce in your school?

c) What methods and policies that are practised at your school would you put an end to and why?

d) How do you feel about Howard Gardner's idea that schools should better reflect the different types of intelligences of all the children at the school? Why/why not? How could that be changed?

e) Think about:

- the lessons taught at your school – how much do they reflect the abilities of all the children?

- the structure of your school and how decisions are made. Put the following in the order that best represents your school. You may add other categories if you wish:

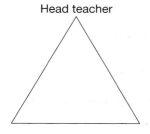

Head teacher

> prefects / younger children / teachers / head boy or girl / head teacher / senior teachers / older children

- the methods used to find the most intelligent pupils, e.g. testing

- whether the traditional subjects are given more prominence at the school.

Then imagine a school:

- *where kids have freedom to be themselves.*
- *where success is not defined by academic achievement but by the child's own definition of success.*
- *where the whole school deals democratically with issues, with each individual having an equal right to be heard.*
- *where you can play all day if you want to, and there is time and space to sit and dream.*

...could there be such a school?

A.S. Neil's Summerhill School

How would you feel about going to a school like Summerhill?

How much do you agree or disagree with the ideas of Summerhill School?

Focus on grammar

The imperative

The imperative is made up of the verb in the infinitive without the use of **to**, and without a subject (e.g. he, they):

- **Talk** about the following.
- **Match** the word and the picture.
- **Listen** and write the words.
- **Look** at the sentences and **decide** if they are true or false.

We use the imperative:

- To give direct orders: **Come here at once!**
- To give instructions or directions: **Take the first turning on the right.**
- To make an invitation: **Come and have a coffee.**
- In signs and notices: **Do not use.**
- For informal advice or information: **Take an umbrella.**
- To warn somebody: **Don't smoke in here!**
- To ask somebody to do something: **Pick it up, please.**

3 Look at the following pictures and imagine what the people are saying. Use the imperative form in each of the sentences.

4 Imagine that somebody is coming from another school and joining yours (like the twins at St Clare's). What advice would you give them so that they felt comfortable at the school and settled in easily? Give at least six pieces of advice using the imperative. For example:

> Arrive early on the first day so that you can have a look around the school.

Focus on vocabulary

5 So far in this unit we have been looking at schools. We have already seen some vocabulary related to schools (denominational, academic, etc.), but we will now look at some more.

First put the following words into alphabetical order.

Then match the words to their definition on the right.

Word	Definition
Qualifications	Person who works in the administration of the school.
Suspended	For children with learning difficulties.
Tuition	The punishment of being kept in school after hours.
Literacy	To do with numbers.
Numeracy	Room where many people sleep next to each other.
Research	Paper evidence of standard of education.
Remedial	Period in which the school calendar is broken up.
Semester	A system of regular testing.
Detention	The further study of something.
Dormitory	To complete a course of study.
Expelled	Removed from a school permanently.
Registrar	Teaching or training.
Continuous assessment	The ability to read and write.
Graduation	To have temporarily stopped someone from attending classes.

6 Copy and complete these sentences with words from the table.

a) She hasn't been sleeping very well as she has to share the _____ with other girls.

b) He is getting _____ classes because he is struggling a bit in class.

c) The _____ needed for university are more difficult to get now because of the competition.

d) He has been given _____ because he was rude to the teacher.

e) The _____ is the best person to ask if you have a question about your payment of the fees.

f) They have exams in the final _____ of the school year.

g) They are to have a _____ ceremony for the final year.

h) The children have been told to _____ any topic they want for the school newspaper.

i) He will be _____ if he continues to disobey the school rules.

j) She has been _____ from all music lessons until she apologises to the teacher.

k) The level of _____ at the school has really improved.

l) He will need extra _____ in order to keep up with the others.

m) _____ is much fairer than exams for some children.

n) _____ is not a strength of hers and she makes lots of mistakes in her maths.

E Let's write

Using direct and indirect speech in writing

We saw the use of dialogue in the extract on page 4 about the twins:

"I hate being the same as everyone else!" said Pat. "Goodness – if only we were allowed to have what we liked, wouldn't we make everyone stare!"

This is an example of direct speech. If it were to be changed to indirect speech, it would look like this:

Pat said that she hated being the same as everyone else and that if they had been allowed to have what they liked they would have made everybody stare.

1 What do you notice about the change from direct to indirect speech?

Say if the following are true or false:
a) Speech marks are no longer used.
b) The tense of the verb changes backwards.
c) The meaning has changed slightly.
d) There are fewer sentences.
e) More punctuation is used.
f) It is more formal.
g) The exact words have not been used.
h) Different pronouns have been used.
i) The word 'that' has been used.
j) There is a change in the order of the words.

> **Direct speech** is the exact words as spoken by the speaker.
>
> **Indirect speech** reports what was said, and is sometimes known as 'reported speech'. That is why the verbs take on the form of the past – what was said is being reported.

Both types of speech can be used in a piece of writing to add variety and contrast. The writer can influence how the reader 'feels' about the piece they have written by using one or the other.

Using direct speech makes your writing more accessible and informal to the reader because it is as if the characters are speaking from the page.

However, in both types of speech, you need to be aware of the points made in Exercise 1.

2 Remember: don't only use 'said' in your writing. Varying the words you use can make your writing more interesting and give it atmosphere.

Do you know some other words that you could use instead of 'said'? Find 19 in the word search on the next page and write them in your book.

```
D A O S R H W H I S P E R E D A
A N N C E F A O S O E X P X R S
D N O R P S I A D B N A L P E S
O O S A L D S B B B S H T L G U
R U C S I E R O R E D S W A H R
D N R A E A S S U D R E P I U E
E C E S D C K E B V H L H N I D
R E A H P O Y R O Y E L L E D D
E D M O A N E D A W C R A D P S
D F E U L F A N S W E R E D B S
D S D T L I D E T R O P R S E B
B E T E E R G O E C Y U T B G G
S M R D D M B R D B F G O L G Y
L N U P R E P E A T E D L L E E
M T S E A D E M A N D E D M D L
Q U E S T I O N E D E D D R O S
```

3 Write the following sentences in direct speech, including all the necessary punctuation.

a) and neither would I said Isabel let one of the maids light it – or Kay

b) I haven't been to the cinema for ages moaned Peter

c) could I borrow your pen please asked Jane as I have forgotten mine

d) the shops are going to be closed tomorrow exclaimed Jenny and that's the second time this month

e) do you mind if I don't come tonight asked Rosaline as I really don't feel very well

f) the boys have gone off to play football and they've left the house a mess stormed Frank

4 Change the sentences in Exercise 3 into reported speech.

5 You are now going to write something that includes both types of speech.

Think about a dialogue you have heard recently or make one up where two people are talking about school. Write about 200 words and make your piece of writing as interesting as possible.

Remember all the points you have learned.

 F Let's do some research

You are going to look at two international organisations that deal with education.

Choose the one that interests you more and, with a friend, do some research on it.

The questions below are to help you with what you are looking for, but it will be necessary to expand on the information.

Use visuals and illustrations in your project to make it look more interesting.

Remember, you want your readers to be interested in what you have done, so take care in how you present your project and the information in it.

The Comenius programme of the European Commission
- What is it?
- What areas of education does it cover?
- What are its main objectives?
- What are its current priorities?

UNESCO
- What is it?
- What is its mission and vision?
- What is its education programme – Education for All by 2015?
- What are the priorities and initiatives for this?

G Let's learn something new

- There are 22 countries where more than half the population is illiterate (cannot read or write) – 15 of them are in Africa.
- Children in Mali (West Africa) spend only two years in school. More than half of them start working between the ages of 10 and 14.
- Men in central Europe tend not to teach – over 75 per cent of lower secondary school teachers are female.

Unit 2 School issues

A Let's start

1 Look at the following pictures and, with your partner, talk about what you think is happening in each one. Where could this happen? Have you ever seen any of these things happening?

a)

b)

c)

d)

2 Choose a title from the word box to match each of the pictures.

Graffiti / Cheating / Truancy / Disrespect / Bullying / Theft / Rebellion / Illegal substances

3 Then match each of the following paragraphs with one of the titles.

a) He's always rude to the teacher, especially behind her back when she can't see him. He makes rude gestures, pulls faces at her or throws things at her. When she speaks to him he rudely answers her back or just ignores her; I've even heard him swear at her.

b) Whenever they can they write on the walls and desks of the school. The head teacher has warned the whole school about it and has told us to look after school property as if it were our own, but some people just don't care.

c) There is a group of three and they are always picking on the little ones, especially the shy ones who don't answer back. I hate the way they get away with it. Other students are too frightened to say anything to the teachers or their parents.

d) Somebody in the school steals things from people's bags during the breaks. It is mostly money so it can be difficult to find out who does it. Kids really shouldn't bring anything of value to school, which is a shame because it means you can't even trust your own school friends.

e) They pretend they are going to school but as soon as they arrive at the school gates they are off into town, to the park or anywhere. I don't know if the school tells their parents or, if they do, the parents just don't care.

f) This girl just doesn't care! Every day she comes to school wearing something that she knows is not part of the school uniform and no matter how many times she is told to go home and change, she just ignores everyone and does it again.

g) I hate people who cheat in tests at school because it makes fun of those of us who sit down and try to do well in an honest way. It's easy to cheat, but it is not easy to sit down and learn something properly, so I think those people are weak and cowards and have no pride in themselves.

h) They are not allowed to bring things like cigarettes into school but there is always somebody who does. At break time they disappear and do their stuff and come back later stinking of smoke.

4 With your partner, talk about the following:

Have you seen examples of any of the above happening at your school?

Can you think of any other school issues not shown here that you think are a problem at your school?

Talk about each of these issues:
- What happened?
- Who was involved?
- Was the situation sorted out by the school or an adult? Why/why not?
- Did either you or your friend have any involvement in the situation?
- Would the situation have improved if either you or your friend had become involved? Why/why not?

What would you do if you knew one of the situations in Exercise 3 was occurring?

Would you consider adopting 'Peer mediation', as you learnt about in Unit 13 of Coursebook 2? How might this help/not help?

B Let's read 1

We are going to look at one of the issues mentioned above: bullying. First, what is bullying? With your partner, copy and complete the spider diagram with words connected to bullying.

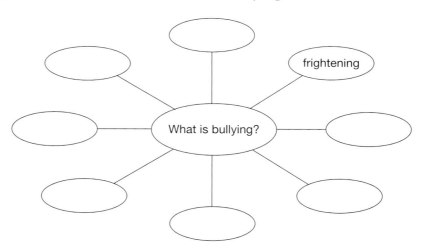

Bullying can be both physical and psychological (mental/emotional).

1 Look at the list on the next page and talk about each point with your friend. Discuss whether you think it is physical or psychological bullying, and copy and complete a table like the one that follows. Give reasons for your answers.

being called horrible names / being threatened / stealing or damaging something that belongs to you / being shoved, kicked or hit / being ignored / being left out of group activities / being laughed at / being spat at / being made to do something you don't want to do / spreading nasty rumours about you in the school

Physical bullying	Psychological bullying

2 We will now look a bit more carefully at what bullying is. Look at the statements below and decide if you agree or disagree with them. Give reasons for your choice.
a) Bullying happens at all schools.
b) Bullying happens with younger and older children.
c) Psychological bullying is not as bad as physical bullying.
d) People who are bullied normally don't tell anyone that it is happening.
e) Bullying happens to all types of children.
f) Any type of child can be a bully.
g) A person who is bullied is weak because they should stand up for themselves.
h) Bullying only happens in the school playground.
i) More boys are bullies than girls.
j) I've seen people at school being bullied.
k) If a person is being bullied they should tell an adult.
l) Bullying is something which should be dealt with and stopped.
m) Bullying can have serious consequences for some children.
n) Bullying is a natural part of school life.

3 You are now going to read an article about a person who was bullied at school, and how they dealt with it.

Look at the points below and find them in the article. Are they true or false?
● The narrator is a girl called Joanne.
● The person who bullied her was a boy.
● The bully practised judo on her.

When the playground becomes a battleground

When Joanne split up with her boyfriend, his new girlfriend started taunting her at school. Before long, she was getting pushed and tripped down stairs, attacked by other pupils and cut off from all her friends.

"I expected it all to blow over and I wanted to handle it myself, but it didn't." she says. "At first I was really scared and didn't want to stand up to her, but as it got bigger and bigger I got more frustrated. And, as I didn't want to let my fear show at school, I'd take it out on my family. I'd come home in a right rage and take it out on everyone just to let a little bit of the frustration out. I couldn't tell her to stop and I felt I was really weak."

Joanne made herself feel better by pushing her little brother around, shouting at her mum and swearing at her father. "I would never reason; would never say sorry for anything." She used anger to cover up her fear so no one would know.

But her mum realised something was wrong. "She said: 'I'm your mum and I'm meant to look after you and I can't look after you if I don't know what's wrong.' I felt guilty and told her. But she wanted to contact the school and the family. I panicked because I thought everyone would say I couldn't fight my own battles."

Her mum made lots of good practical suggestions and Joanne took up judo as a result and tried to stand up for herself more. However, not even good advice from her judo instructor seemed to help and Joanne even told her mum the trouble had stopped.

But she was desperate enough to admit to herself she needed more help. So she booked herself into one of her school's anti-bullying counselling sessions.

Joanne's counsellor was her own age and helped her to think of solutions that suited her; without making her feel the bullying was trivial.

As a result Joanne decided it was time to tell her friends and teacher what was happening. "The more I told people the more I could breathe again. The heaviness in my heart lifted. Eventually loads and loads of people knew and every time the bully started something, someone would be there for me and she would have to leave me alone. The best way of dealing with bullies is to tell your friends and teachers!"

Joanne is much happier now and has qualified as a school counsellor who can help other students facing the same kinds of problems: "I've been through it myself so people know when they talk to me that I understand how they feel."

4 Copy and complete the table with information from the article.

Examples of how Joanne was bullied	The people who Joanne took her frustration out on	Ways Joanne's mother wanted her to deal with the bullying

Features of the counsellor	Actions taken by Joanne after the counselling	Positive aspects that came out of Joanne's counselling

5 In your own words, explain the following expressions from the article.

split up	take it out on
cut off	cover up
blow over	took up
stand up	

 C # Let's speak and listen

1 Look at the following situations. How would you and your friend deal with them? For each situation think of at least **three** ways to resolve the situation.

a) My name's Arzu. I stopped going into school on some days because I was having difficulty reading and the other children would start making fun of me. So I would lie to my parents and tell them I was at school, but instead I used to sit in the park and only go to school for the lessons that I liked or was good at.

b) My name's Pedro. My maths teacher used to make fun of me and call me Pedro the donkey in front of the other children. He would make me sit at the back of the class and never used to come and give me any help. I started doing really badly in maths but I didn't know who could help me.

c) I went past our school over the weekend and saw these kids there who I know from Year 7. Some were playing football in the school grounds but others I saw were spraying paint over the walls, which have recently been painted. I'm frightened to tell anyone in case they find out that it was me who told the teachers.

d) There's this girl in our class who I've seen stealing from other pupils' bags. When she saw me watching her she started crying and said her mother couldn't give her any money for lunch as they are poor. I felt really guilty and didn't say anything to anyone but I told her not to do it again because it's wrong to steal. She said she wouldn't but things have gone missing again and I don't know what to do.

2 Now listen to the counsellor talking about each situation. Copy the following table and make a note of the advice they give in each case. One example has been given. How is the advice the same as or different from yours?

	Situation a	Situation b	Situation c	Situation d
Your solutions				
The counsellor's solutions	Stop telling lies to her parents and talk to them instead.			

D Let's read 2

1 Look at the names and numbers below and see if they mean anything to you.

Louisiana Technical College – 3
E.O. Green School – 1
Northern Illinois University – 6
Central High School – 1

They were all involved in shootings in the year 2008. The figure is the number of fatalities (pupils killed).

2 What do you know about school shootings? Are the following true or false?
  ● They have only happened in America.
  ● The perpetrator (doer) often kills themself as well.
  ● The perpetrator will usually just shoot anybody.
  ● There is no one type of person who would be a perpetrator.
  ● The perpetrators are often people who have been 'isolated' from their peers.
  ● Nearly all school shootings are done by male students.
  ● Many schools now have security checks at all entrances.

3 School shootings are on the increase and there could be many reasons for this. Look at the suggested reasons below and decide if you agree or disagree with them. Can you suggest any other reasons?

	🙂	🙁
They are the result of a more violent society.		
Guns are easily bought in the United States.		
Students are not given enough individual attention.		
Students learn how to be killers from the internet and TV.		
Society 'idealises' (romanticises) the idea of killing.		
Teenagers can't always distinguish between reality and fiction.		
Teenagers are frustrated because military service no longer exists in most countries.		
Often both parents are out at work.		
Families are smaller and there is less guidance and support for young adults.		
There is more pressure on young people than in the past.		
Children are pushed to achieve more than in the past.		
Standards at school are much higher, which increases the pressures at school.		
Teenagers demand more and get frustrated when they don't get what they want.		

4 Now read the text below.

Teen violence and school shootings – facts

- TV influences behaviour.
- Violence on TV occurs in most programs and especially in cartoons (five times more).
- Thousands of studies have shown that violence on TV influences behaviour and attitudes among children who watch it.
- Aggressive behaviour in children is linked to those who view violent TV shows.
- TV violence is linked to the proliferation (increase) of violence in our culture.
- By the age of 12, the average child has witnessed at least 8000 murders and more than 100 000 other acts of violence on TV.
- Children spend more time in front of the TV than they do in the classroom.
- The proliferation of violence on the internet has become a huge factor in desensitising children to violence and crimes against women, children and vulnerable minorities.
- The army uses video games to train their people in the use of firearms.
- The 14-year-old killer in the Paducah, Kentucky school shooting had never fired a real pistol in his life. Nevertheless, he fired eight shots; five of them head shots, the other three upper torso shots, killing eight children.

Focus on grammar

The present perfect

5 Find the following examples of the present perfect in the text above:
- have shown
- has witnessed
- has become

The present perfect is formed with:

have/has + past participle

With regular verbs, the past participle is formed by adding -ed / -d / -ied to the verb, e.g. walk – walked / change – changed / marry – married.

With irregular verbs, the form changes, e.g. find – found / buy – bought.

The present perfect is used in the following situations:

- When something happened in the past but still affects us now, e.g.

   Thousands of studies have shown that violence …

   The studies were done in the past but the results of the studies are still being looked at today.

- When something started in the past and continues in the present, e.g.

   The proliferation of violence on the internet has become …

   The proliferation continues today.

- When we use words like: ever, never, just, always, only, still, since, etc., e.g.

   I've just finished my lunch, thank you.

6 Re-order the following words, and make changes where necessary, to create sentences in the present perfect.
a) France / he / never / has / be / to
b) to / things / they / try / improve / fail / but / have
c) children / visit / never / museum / the / have / the
d) long / Sara / Rome / has / study / how / in ?
e) drive / 300 km / I / today / have
f) go / Eiffel Tower / have / ever / up / the / you ?
g) new / find / job / a / Peter / has
h) uniform / she / got / her / school / ready / has ?
i) new / the / are / have / children / arrive / classroom / in / the / and
j) tickets / the / sell / all / out / have

7 Write six sentences using the present perfect explaining why you think school shootings have increased worldwide, e.g.

   Children have taken the idea from television because it looks exciting.

Focus on vocabulary

Abbreviations

Here are some abbreviations from this section:

- TV = television
- e.g. = for example.
- etc. = and so on.

There are different ways of using abbreviations and this can often make it confusing for the user. However, what is important is that you are consistent in how you use them.

- If the first letter of the word is a capital, then the first letter in the abbreviation should also be a capital: *United Nations = UN*.
- If the first letter isn't a capital, then lower case is used: *a.m./am = ante meridian (before noon)*
- Full stops are sometimes used but not always, so *9 am* or *9 a.m.* would both be acceptable.
- To form the plural form of the abbreviation, just add an 's' in the lower case: *CDs/TVs*, etc.
- An apostrophe is only added to the plural form to avoid confusion, e.g. *the x's and y's of the chromosomes.*

8 Find the abbreviations or full words for the following. Use a dictionary or the internet to help you.

British Broadcasting Corporation	No.
North Atlantic Treaty Organisation	Independent Television
United Arab Emirates	RSVP
Organisation of Petroleum Exporting Countries	National Aeronautics and Space Administration
account	UFO
Doctor	W.C.
p.m.	GCSE
DVD	dept.
PTO	General Headquarters
PM	kg.

E Let's write

Recognising the opinion of the writer

If we look at the text in 'Let's read 2' on page 23, we can tell by their choice of words that the writer is trying to get across a subject which they feel strongly and negatively about.

For example:

proliferation	14-year-old <u>killer</u>
desensitising	<u>thousands</u> of studies
aggressive	

All of those words/expressions are used to give the reader a negative feel about the issue, and for them to be influenced by the writer's stance (position).

Other features of a text may include the following:
- The nationality of the writer.
- If it is written in the first person, the writer is attempting to speak directly to the reader and can give the text more of an 'alive' feeling.
- If it is written in the third person, the writer is describing the events from the outside and there is a more distant tone.
- The cultural background of the writer.
- Who the writer wants to interest.

1   We are going to look at both of the texts from the reading sections in this unit and see how much we can understand about the writers. Copy and complete the following. Text 2 has been done as an example.

	Text 1	Text 2
1 Nationality of writer		1 American – uses an example from Kentucky in text and spells 'programme' *program*.
2 Grammatical form used to influence reader		2 The passive – *is linked* – and 3rd person, which both make the text more formal and distant.
3 Cultural background of writer		3 Educated as has good vocabulary, e.g. *proliferation/ desensitising* and doesn't use any slang or dialect.
4 Audience text is aimed at		4 Aimed at adults because of the type of information.
5 Purpose of text		5 To inform and influence opinion of reader.
6 Other		

2 Rewrite the text in 'Let's read 2' from the position of a teenager who enjoys TV and video games and doesn't believe that they influence children. For example:

- TV influences behaviour.

  TV can influence a child's behaviour in many ways – both positive and negative.

F Let's do some research

'Disrespect' is something that varies from culture to culture. What is disrespectful to one culture might not be disrespectful to another. Examples would be:

- Saying thank you, please, excuse me, etc., is a normal and polite way of speaking to someone in British culture. But in some Mediterranean cultures these terms are not used as much.
- If a school child is slouching in their chair in a classroom, it might be considered disrespectful to the teacher in some cultures. However, in other cultures this behaviour may be perfectly acceptable.

Now think about other forms of disrespect or maybe look at your own environment for your research. Can you think of at least **four** examples?

For each example talk about the following:
a) the respectful or disrespectful act
b) the cultures involved
c) why and how it would be considered disrespectful
d) the age groups it would be disrespectful to.

G Let's learn something new

- Surveys have shown that theft is the most serious crime in American schools.
- In the United Kingdom truancy has increased by half a million lessons since 1999. That's now about 1.4 million missed lessons every year!
- It's a fact that larger schools (with more than 1500 students) have more discipline problems. More than 700 students a year are permanently excluded from schools in the UK.

Unit 3 Higher education

A Let's start

1 Look at the following words and discuss, with a friend, what each one means. Then divide the words into the three categories shown in the table below. Talk about the words you don't know with your teacher.

Freshers	University
Degree	College
MA	Sixth-form college
MBA	International Baccalaureate
BSc	Tutor
BA	Lecturer
Vocational	Qualifications
Undergraduate	Apprentice
Post-graduate	Tertiary

Words I know	Words I'm not sure about	Words I don't know

2 With your partner, talk about the education system in your country, and complete a table with information. Use the points in the diagram below to help you.

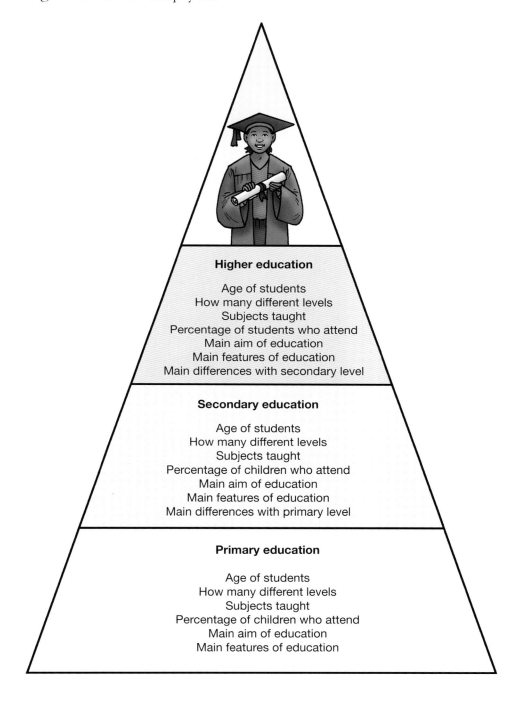

Higher education

Age of students
How many different levels
Subjects taught
Percentage of students who attend
Main aim of education
Main features of education
Main differences with secondary level

Secondary education

Age of students
How many different levels
Subjects taught
Percentage of children who attend
Main aim of education
Main features of education
Main differences with primary level

Primary education

Age of students
How many different levels
Subjects taught
Percentage of children who attend
Main aim of education
Main features of education

3 With your partner, talk about the advantages and disadvantages of higher education. Think about why you feel it is necessary or not necessary to go on to higher education.

Reasons to go into higher education	Reasons not to go into higher education

4 Look at the following reasons and put them into the correct category. Are any of them the same as the reasons you talked about with your partner?

- You are less likely to be unemployed through your life.
- You will earn on average 35 per cent more than the average person.
- Nobody in your family has gone on to higher education.
- You don't have the confidence to succeed.
- You will need to start earning a salary to help your family.
- You won't be able to afford the costs of higher education.
- More courses are now offered than in the past.
- There are more universities and colleges than ever before.
- You could combine work with higher education.
- More opportunities will be opened to you in life.
- The experience of higher education will make your life richer.
- You have had enough of learning and want to go into the real world and work.

B Let's read 1

1 How do you think life at university or college is different from going to school? With your partner, think of at least six differences and six similarities. Copy and complete a table like the one below. One suggestion has already been given.

Similarities	Differences
I would be with people of the same age.	

2 Now look at the statements below about how life at university or college will be and decide if you agree or disagree with them.
- I will have to be more responsible for the work I do.
- More time will be spent on research and self-study.
- I will have more free time.
- There will not be such strict deadlines for when homework is to be returned.
- There will be fewer academic pressures.
- Lecturers and tutors will be like the teachers at school.
- Studying will be easier because I'm doing subjects that I want.
- There won't be as many tests as at school.
- Learning will be more of a two-way process between the student and the lecturer.
- I will be expected to participate more in the lectures and give my opinion.
- I will no longer be spoon-fed and will have to decide what I need to learn.
- I can argue with the lecturers if I don't agree with something they're saying.
- I will meet a lot of different people.

3 If you were to go into higher education, how would your everyday life be different from what it is now? What would you need to learn to do that you don't do now?

With your partner, think about the different things your parents do for you at home that are a necessary part of your everyday life. Copy the table below and write your ideas in the first column. Then complete the second column with information that you would need to learn about and do if you were to go into higher education.

Things my parents do for me now	Things I would need to learn how to do if I were to go into higher education
• Wash my clothes.	• Learn to write a cheque or how to use a credit card.

4 You are now going to read an article on the following page about the change from school to university. Read it once and find at least four points that are mentioned in Exercise 2.

The transition from school to university

One of the hardest tasks for freshers is to get to grips with the way uni differs from school. It can be a shock when teachers start being really pleased if you answer back, and you don't have to hand in your homework for weeks and weeks!

Like anything in life, preparation will help. This means talking to existing students on your course as well as to friends and family, making sure they feel included in this exciting new step in your life and that they realise how much you will value their support. Preparation for your new life should also extend to learning a few life skills before you start at uni, such as being able to boil an egg, read a bank statement and put the right amount of bleach down a toilet!

One of the first things you should do when you first start is to walk around and identify all the buildings relevant to you to make you feel a full part of your new community. Also, join a society, seminar or bus queue as soon as possible so you can start making friends. It is much harder to join things later in the term.

However, do make sure you know what is expected of you when it comes to academic work – and what you should be expecting from tutors. Don't forget that they won't yet know how capable you are, so it's up to you to make an impression, and to ask if you don't understand something. No one will think you are stupid, though they might get irritated if they've just sent you an email explaining everything. One of the biggest differences from school is that teachers won't keep nagging you about deadlines, or even tell you how many hours of study you should be doing. Instead, you will have to work all this out for yourself. You'll need to learn to prioritise and leave plenty of time for assignments, especially at the beginning so that you can work out where to find things like books.

The most important thing is not to rush things, nor expect too much from friends – or yourself – too soon. And remember, even if you ignore all advice, nobody is going to give you a detention!

5 Complete a spider diagram with information from the passage. At the centre of the diagram, write 'Advice from the writer'. Summarise eight pieces of advice that the writer gives.

6 There is a mistake about the passage in each of the sentences below. Find the mistake and correct it.
- Detention is given if you ignore all advice.
- You don't need to make an impression because tutors know what you are capable of.
- It is rude to answer back to teachers.
- The teachers ask for the homework for weeks and weeks.
- Family and friends value the support.

- You will be asked to boil an egg at university.
- Walking will make you feel part of the community.
- Making friends should be left till later in the term.
- You will be thought of as stupid if you don't know something.
- Teachers will nag you about how many hours of studying you should do.

  # Let's speak and listen

1 Talk about the following with your partner:
   - What are vocational and academic subjects?
   - How are they different?
   - How might courses you study at university be different from those that you might study at a college?
   - What jobs would require a university degree?
   - What jobs would require a vocational qualification?
   - How might a vocational qualification be better than a university degree?
   - How might a university degree be better than a vocational degree?

2 Look at the following jobs/careers and decide if you think they would need a vocational qualification or a university degree:

Chef	Lawyer	Journalist
Dentist	Supervisor	Graphic designer
Engineer	Lecturer	Air cabin crew
Electrician	School nurse	Train driver
Teacher	Air traffic controller	Police officer
Plumber	Architect	Soldier
Legal clerk	Civil servant	Engineer
Surgeon	Computer system analyst	Accountant
Secretary	Archeologist	

Vocational qualification	University degree

3 What are the most popular courses studied at university? Look at the pie chart and try to match the subjects with the percentage that shows their popularity.

The pie chart shows what subjects students study in higher education in the United Kingdom.

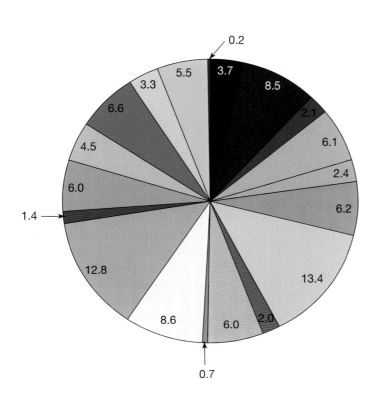

Medicine and dentistry
Subjects connected to medicine
Biological sciences
Veterinary sciences
Agriculture and related subjects
Physical sciences
Mathematical sciences
Computer science
Engineering and technology
Architecture, building and planning
Social studies
Law
Business and administrative studies
Mass communications and
    documentation
Languages
Historical and philosophical studies
Creative arts and design
Education
Combined subjects

4 Now listen to the person who did the research and find out if you were correct.

5 With your partner, talk about how things are different in your country. Do you think the same subjects are studied? Are they just as popular?

D Let's read 2

We have been looking at different courses and jobs, but what else is involved in going to college or university?

Education, we saw, was one of the most popular courses studied at college and/or university, so we will look a bit more closely at that. First, it would be a good idea to talk to your teachers at school.

1 What do you know about teachers and teaching?

With your partner, talk about the following subjects:
- qualifications
- salary
- hours of work
- holidays
- competition (how difficult it is to find jobs)
- future prospects (opportunities to move on or up)
- job satisfaction (how happy teachers are with their jobs).

2 Now think about six questions that you and your partner could ask your teachers about their college or university life.

3 You will find 12 more questions in the word circle below – are they the same as yours?

4 Now read the passage below.

Can you find answers to the questions in Exercise 3?

Jobs in education and training

Those who work in education and training give a wide range of people of all ages and backgrounds the opportunity to learn and develop throughout their lives.

- *Many of those in education have a professional role as a teacher or lecturer. Teachers work with pupils and young people aged from four to 19. Lecturers may work in further education, where they are teaching students aged 16 or over, or in higher education, where they are working with students studying vocational or university courses.*
- *Trainers help people to acquire the skills and knowledge that they need in their working lives, and those working in lifelong learning also help adults to make the most of their leisure time.*

The work environment varies from job to job, but most work takes place in classrooms, lecture theatres and training areas. Some is based outdoors. Administrative staff are likely to be office based. Many people in this sector work around 37 hours a week from Monday to Friday, but some teaching jobs require evening and weekend work.

For most jobs in this sector it is important to enjoy working with people. Spoken and written communication skills are vital, and a thorough knowledge of specific subjects is often essential. Motivational skills and the ability to give constructive criticism are important in teaching and training. Good organisational skills are relevant to many jobs.

People usually need a degree or postgraduate qualification to teach in schools. Life experience is more important than qualifications for some other jobs, such as learning counsellors.

Continuing professional development is essential for teachers through on-the-job training or further qualifications, and this will help towards any promotion routes. There may also be opportunities to work overseas.

Focus on grammar

The present tenses

5 Find two examples from the passage above that show the present simple. Then find another two examples that show the present continuous.

6 In the table below, match the use of the tenses to the examples given.

Use	Example
The present simple	
a) A permanent state or situation b) For facts c) For repeated actions and events d) For scheduled events in the near future e) Some verbs normally take the simple form	i) The bus leaves at 5.30 so don't miss it. ii) They come home on the bus every day. iii) Do they understand me? iv) I live in the capital city. v) The sun rises in the east.
The present continuous	
f) For something happening now g) Longer actions happening now h) For future plans i) Repetition and irritation with 'always'/'constantly'	vi) We're spending the holidays in Vienna. vii) I'm eating my lunch! viii) She's always borrowing money from me! ix) She's studying French at school.

7 Match each of the sentences below with one of the uses given above.
- She always forgets her purse.
- She is constantly talking in class.
- She cooks dinner every night.
- They are listening to the radio.
- Lessons start at 7.45 every day.
- Aren't you teaching at the new school now?
- I'm meeting the head teacher later.
- Paper is made from wood.

8 Think of suitable verbs to complete these sentences. Put the verb into either the present simple or the present continuous.

I really _____ my grandparents but it is such a long way to visit every time.

He is _____ the window which you broke yesterday.

They _____ every day at 12.00 but he is always late.

I'm _____ on the phone so please be quiet!

She _____ in a kitchen all day and it is very hard work.

A baker _____ the bread early each morning before people _____.

The cockerel _____ every morning and wakes me up.

She _____ to school today as she doesn't _____ very well.

I _____ that all students should be made to wear school uniform.

He _____ to apologise for being rude to the teacher so I have given him detention.

Focus on vocabulary

Writing numbers

In the text on page 36 we see the numbers: four, 16, 19 and 37.

9 Why is it that the number four is written as a word but the others are written as digits? Find the answer below.

Here are some rules for writing numbers in passages.
- When a number like twenty-one is written, the hyphen joins the two words together and the word would be counted as one word.
- Any numbers written from one to nine are normally written as a word; 10 and beyond are written as digits. This is especially true when a number is used with a noun, e.g. nine children.
- With measurements a digit is used, e.g. 2 kilometres, 7 centimetres, etc. But the single abbreviated form is used even if the number makes the word plural, e.g. 2 km, 7 cm.
- The % sign is not used when writing – the word itself is used instead, e.g. '25 per cent of the class' not '25% of the class'.
- In American English the date is written differently from British English. In American English the order is month/day/year, e.g. 12/31/2010. In British English it is day/month/year, e.g. 31/12/2010. Also in British English, ordinal numbers are more common, e.g. 31st December 2010.
- Use a hyphen when the number is changed by the noun, e.g. a 10-inch hole, a 20-kilo bag. Again, the measurement is in the singular form.
- Use words when describing a form of measurement, e.g. She ate a kilo of sugar.
- You should begin a sentence with a number written out, e.g. 'Twenty-three children left the park' not '23 children left the park'.

- We usually use numbers for:
  a) writing an address – the house number and postcode have digits, e.g.
     23 Park Lane
     London SW21
  b) money, e.g. €20 or £20
  c) time, e.g. 9.15 a.m. or 12 o'clock
  d) talking about a year, e.g. In 1945 the Second World War ended.

10 Find the mistake in the following sentences and correct them.
- Three Oak Tree Lane
- The screen is 80 cms long.
- That will cost forty dollars, please.
- They arrive on January 23.
- 14 people were killed in the fires.
- The play begins at eight thirty, so please be on time.
- There were only 2 books left on the shelf.
- About 55% of the world's population is made up of women.
- They had walked only 1 km before they realised they were lost.
- He joined our school in nineteen ninety-nine.

11 Now write the following as if they were part of a passage. Write the answers in full sentences.

For example, The date you were born – I was born on _____.
a) The date you were born
b) How much you weigh (roughly)
c) How much it costs to buy a bottle of water
d) Your full address
e) The time you leave home to go to school each day
f) The number of children in your class
g) The percentage of girls and boys in your class
h) The distance from your home to your school
i) The size of your *International English 3* Coursebook
j) The postcode of your address

 Let's write

Informal writing

1 Look at the text in 'Let's read 1' on page 32 and answer the following questions.

- Who has it been written for?
- Where would you expect to find a piece of writing like this?
- Would you say it is an informal or formal piece of writing? Why? Informal writing is a piece of writing that you would do for a friend, family member or for an audience that you want to feel comfortable and friendly towards.

2 The above explains why the passage in 'Let's read 1' is informal. Find examples of the following that the passage uses to have an informal tone:

- abbreviations
- exclamation marks
- contractions
- friendly style.

3 Think about other places where informal and formal language would be more appropriate. Copy and complete the table with your ideas.

Formal language	Informal language
At school towards the head teacher and teachers.	

Other examples of informal writing:

- 'I' instead of 'you' is more commonly used.
- The passive form is not used, e.g. 'Teachers will collect the papers.' rather than 'The papers will be collected by the teachers.'
- Phrasal verbs and colloquial expressions are more likely to be used, e.g. 'He <u>ran off</u> with my bag but that was <u>OK</u> as there was nothing in it.'
- More common everyday words are used, e.g. 'We'll be leaving <u>soon</u>.' rather than 'We will be leaving <u>presently</u>.'
- Shorter simpler sentences are used instead of more complex ones, e.g. 'The cat is sitting on the mat.' rather than 'The amazingly regal cat is sitting on the front door mat.'

4 Look at the letter below which has been written to a student named Alex Trasmundi. The letter is from his head teacher concerning some unauthorised days taken off. Rewrite the letter with the more informal words and expressions given below. Change only the formality and not the content of the letter and imagine that it has been written by a head teacher who has a friendly relationship with the students at his school.

thanks / about / Michael / quick / talk about / got / tell / fits / asap / so / subjects / I'm waiting for / for you / re / talk about / come to / some / for everyone / be thankful / speak to / subject / also / are there / answer

21 January 2009

Dear Mr Alex Trasmundi

Thank you for your letter, which we received on the 23rd October 2009.

There are a number of issues that we would like to discuss with you concerning the letter which your parents supposedly wrote on your behalf regarding your absence from school for the two days last week.

I would appreciate it if you would inform us at the earliest opportunity when you would be able to attend a meeting where we can discuss the issue. Furthermore, I would like to stress how important it is that your parents are present at the meeting. Therefore, I would ask that you communicate with them and arrange a date that is suitable for all parties.

I await your prompt reply.

Respectfully yours

Michael Makario

Mr Michael Makario

F Let's do some research

You are going to research a college or university that you might be interested in attending at some point in the future. To do this, think about the following:

- the subjects you enjoy studying at school and why you enjoy them
- what, if anything, you would like to do in the future
- what subjects you would like to study at college or university
- what qualifications you would need to get into the college/university
- what qualifications you would need for your future career
- how long the courses are
- how much the fees are
- where the college or university is
- whether it would be possible to work as well as study
- whether you would study from home or live at the college/university
- any other information you think is necessary for your research.

G Let's learn something new

- The word 'university' comes from the Latin word *universus*, meaning 'the whole' or 'entire'.
- The University of Constantinople (now known as Istanbul), which was founded in 425 AD, was considered the first institution of higher learning.
- The first degree-granting universities in Europe were: The University of Bologna (Italy) 1088; the University of Paris c. 1150; the University of Oxford (UK) 1167; and the University of Cambridge (UK) 1209.

Unit 4 — Money makes the world go round!

A Let's start

1 What do you know about money? Look at the following pictures and with your partner make a sentence about each one.

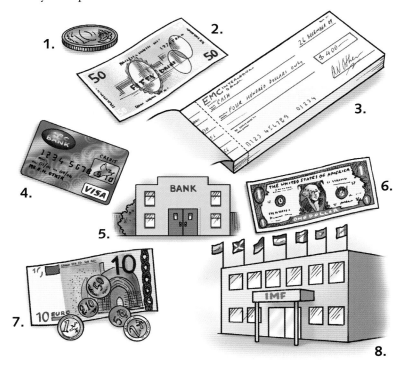

2 Now match the sentences below to each of the pictures. There are two sentences for each picture.

a) You write the amount you want paid on this.

b) This is a place where people deposit their money.

c) In 2002 bank notes and coins were first introduced for this currency.

d) The first president of the United States, George Washington, is printed on this.

e) Signing for the amount is now being replaced by a PIN (Personal Identification Number).

f) The first ones were made about 2700 years ago by the Lydians (now Turkey).

g) It is a crime for anyone to copy or print one.

h) This is an international organisation set up to promote monetary co-operation between countries.

i) It is the currency of the United States.

j) This currency is the same in 15 European countries.

k) This is made from plastic and has an electronic chip on it.

l) These are becoming outdated and being replaced by electronic forms of payment.

m) The metal from which they are made has no value.

n) This is where money is kept safe.

o) A Government issues these and guarantees their value.

p) It has a membership of 185 countries.

3 How did money come about? Where was money first used?

Find the answers to the above questions and more in the exercise below. Match the phrases in columns A and B to form sentences.

Date	A	B
9000–6000 BC	Exchange of animals and plant products was used …	… Lydia to Greece.
c. 3000–2000 BC	The first concept of banking was developed in Mesopotamia by …	… paper money being issued.
c. 1000 BC	In China mock shells were produced and …	… bank notes as the official form of exchange.
687 BC	The first true coins were produced in …	… as a form of payment called barter.
c. 600–530 BC	The use of coins spread rapidly from …	… Lydia.
30 BC	The Romans introduced …	… used as money.
9–15 AD	A shortage of copper in China resulted in …	… adopted in the US.
1400	The first …	… exchanged over the Internet.
1792	The dollar was …	… banks were founded.
1931	Gold was abandoned and exchanged for …	… taxes and pure gold and silver coins.
Now	Electronic money is …	… storing things safely in temples and palaces.

B Let's read 1

1

What do you know about the game Monopoly? What is a monopoly?

> The word *monopoly* comes from the Greek meaning *alone* or *single* + *to sell*. A monopoly is when an individual or enterprise is the only one offering a service or product, with no competitors.

Look at the statements about the game of Monopoly and with your partner decide if they are true or false.

- Monopoly can be played by adults and children.
- Monopoly is a game about money.
- It is a game about buying and selling properties.
- It has the names of places in Britain round the board.
- You can go to jail in Monopoly.
- You play with one dice and move round the board.
- You collect money by renting and selling your properties.
- The person with the most money and properties is the winner.
- It is one of the most popular games in the world.
- There is an internet version of the game.
- Everybody starts with the same amount of money.
- Every time you pass 'GO' you collect some money.

2 You are now going to play a type of Monopoly game but with words connected to money and economics. The board has been laid out on the following page. The rules of the game are as follows:

You play with your partner to find the answers.

You may use a dictionary to help you.

You can only move forward one step at a time and only after you have found the correct word from the centre of the board.

You go to jail and start again if you don't know any of the words.

The first people in your class to finish are the winners.

START → FINISH	Different values of money	Where a bank saves your money	When you add more money to your account	When you take money out of your account	Money given by the bank for saving your money
When a government spends more money than it has					Money borrowed from the bank
To put money into a project with the hope of gain					A written promise of payment
A measure of national income					A returned cheque because there is no money in the account
The buyers					Electronic bank
The value of one foreign exchange against the other	The making of extra money in business	Rise in the level of prices	Internationalisation of the economy	Your computer connected to the bank's computer	JAIL

The International English 3 Money Game

ATM (Automatic Teller Machine) · Profit · Inflation · On line banking · Savings account · Denominations · GDP · Budget deficit · Cheque · Deposit · Globalisation · Loan · Bounced cheque · Investment · Exchange rate · Interest · Consumers · Withdrawal

3 You are now going to read about the game of Monopoly.

Monopoly board game players can now pay for properties with debit cards

The internationally-known game Monopoly has been published in 26 languages and in 80 countries around the world. Since being introduced in 1935, an estimated half a billion people have played it. It has taught the multitudes what they think they know about how the economy works. Whether the game reflects the true economy or not is disputed as players become owners of land, houses and hotels, giving them the feeling of power and control over their losing gaming partners. The acquisition of property is not through any entrepreneurship but through the luck in the number rolled by the die.

Despite the 'unreality' of the game, its popularity has remained and adaptations have been made to keep up with the times. Not only do the names of the places on the game change depending on where it is being played and sold, but also the game makers Parker have phased out the standard multi-coloured cash in a new version and instead players will use a Visa mock debit card to keep track of how much they win or lose. The card is inserted into an electronic machine where the banker taps in cardholders' earnings and payments.

Parker said the replacing of cash with plastic showed the game was moving with the times, as the new electronic Monopoly reflects the changing nature of society and the advancement of technology.

The new version follows a survey of 2056 adults which showed 70% used cash less than they did a decade ago.

It is part of an international deal between Parker and finance giant Visa, which designed the mock debit card and its electronic machine.

4 Answer the following questions about the passage.
   a) What research did the game makers Parker do before deciding to change the game?
   b) Which two organisations cooperated to make the changes to the game?
   c) For about how long has the game been around?
   d) Does the writer feel that players learn how an economy is run? Why/why not?
   e) What three things does the winner need to buy in order to win?
   f) What does the passage suggest is the normal way to become a property owner?
   g) In which language would Monopoly be played in Mexico and Argentina?

h) In which language is Monopoly played in your country?

i) Would you say that people used cash or debit cards more in your country?

j) Find words in the passage where the meanings are similar to the following:

i) ten years	**iii)** industrialist	**v)** argued
ii) not real	**iv)** approximate	**vi)** obtaining/buying

 ## C Let's speak and listen

1 With a partner, do the following. You can ask your teacher to help you.

a) Copy the table below. Then find out the average salary and household expenses in your country and complete the column 'You'.

b) Listen to Mark talking about how much things cost in his country and complete the details in his column.

c) In the final column, find out what your currency's exchange rate is compared to the dollar and calculate your income and expenditure in dollars.

	You	Mark	$
Weekly income:			
Rent/mortgage			
School fees			
Food and vegetables			
Petrol and transportation costs			
Utility bills (e.g. electricity, water, etc.)			
Other expenses (list them), e.g. • entertainment • clothes			
Total expenses:			
How much income have you got left?			
What currency have you worked in?			
What, if any, are the differences between your costs and those of Mark?			
If there is a difference between your income and expenditure, decide on the following with your friend: • If there is a deficit, what are your options? • If you have more income than expenses, what would you do with the excess income?			

D Let's read 2

1 With a partner, talk about the different places you go shopping for food, clothes, electrical goods, etc. Make a list of the names of places where you shop.

What is internet shopping?

Can you name any companies that offer internet shopping?

With your partner, talk about how internet shopping and traditional shopping are the same or different.

Internet shopping v traditional shopping	
The same	**Different**
They both use credit cards.	

2 Now discuss the advantages and disadvantages of internet shopping compared with traditional shopping. Write down your findings in a table like the one below.

Internet shopping	
Advantages	**Disadvantages**

3 Look at the list of ideas below. Decide if they offer suggestions about the advantages or disadvantages of internet shopping. How many of them are the same as or different from your ideas?
- There are no queues.
- Security worries about using credit cards over the internet.
- Time can be saved as not driving or walking to shop.
- It is difficult and expensive if you want to return a product to the company.
- Saves money on petrol and parking costs.
- Smaller companies can compete with larger ones.
- You can't try clothes, etc. on first.
- You don't get to see the products before you buy them.
- Quick and easy to shop around looking for best bargains.
- You can shop 24 hours a day.
- Internet companies will have all your personal details.
- You can shop internationally.
- You have a large selection of products to buy.
- Easier for people with young children or the old.
- Sometimes products can get lost in the post.

4 What are the different stages you go through when you shop on the internet? Look at the list of stages below. What is the correct order for the stages?

Different stages of internet shopping:
a) Choose method of payment
b) Place your order
c) Enter your password
d) View products
e) Go to the checkout
f) Confirm your order
g) Receive e-receipt
h) Select products to buy
i) Put products in your trolley/basket
j) Confirm your address for delivery.

5 Now read this article about internet shopping.

Internet shopping: High street stores are losing out to independents online

Established high street retailers are losing out to internet-savvy rivals because they are not very good at marketing themselves online, according to a report out today.

A survey showed that some high street stores' marketing is so ineffective they are difficult to find through a Google search and business is therefore being lost to small, independent retailers.

In June there were over 19.3m individual searches for laptops in the UK. The results of those searches were dominated by 10 websites, which between them secured 81.2% of all the traffic. Of those, PC World was the only established UK high street retailer to appear, at number six, with 4.7% of the search traffic.

"We are not surprised by these figures," said a representative of the survey team. "Across the retailing sectors we are seeing established retailers, with significant marketing budgets, fail to make an impact in internet search. They are still failing to understand how to market themselves online, and as a result are losing significant revenues to independent and internet-savvy retailers."

It is believed that, rather than hire someone to optimise search engine techniques, companies were spending that revenue on advertising, despite the fact that 91% of internet users prefer using their own search results.

UK online spending was worth £46.6bn last year, up 54% on the previous year. This is because it is believed that people "were trying to shop more carefully".

Focus on grammar

The passive

Remember how the passive is formed:

form of verb 'to be' + past participle, e.g.

The Ferrari car is built by the Italians.

It is used:

a) when the action is more important than the doer
b) when the person or thing doing the action is unknown
c) in formal English
d) in technical English to explain how to do something.

6 Find examples of the following passive forms in the text opposite:
- Continuous tense form
- Simple present tense form
- Simple present negative tense form
- Past tense form

7 Explain why the passive has been used so much in the passage about internet shopping.

8 Look at the cheque and imagine that your friend has never written one before. Write instructions on 'How to write a cheque', using the passive where necessary.

```
┌─────────────────────────────────────────────────────────┐
│ EMC BANK                            Date:                 │
│     INTERNATIONAL                                         │
│ Pay: [Name]                                               │
│                                     ┌───────────────────┐ │
│                                     │ [Amount in numbers]│ │
│ [Amount in words]                   └───────────────────┘ │
│                                          59611503         │
│                                          A.N. Other       │
│                                                           │
│                                          [Signature]      │
│ 140408 4512 0736 5911503                                  │
└─────────────────────────────────────────────────────────┘
```

9 Change the tenses of the passive verbs in the passage on page 50: present → past, or past → present. Then make affirmative sentences negative, and the negative sentences affirmative.

10 Copy the table below and complete it by changing the sentences from the passive to active, or active to passive.

Active	Passive
The class read the book in one week.	
You must finish everything first.	
	The computer was rebooted by Khan.
The girls wrote the nicest stories.	
The Chinese won the most medals.	
	The letter was sent out to all the parents by the secretary.
	The car is being serviced tomorrow.
The children broke the window.	
Someone will collect the essays later.	
Mum baked the cake last night.	
	The book has been bought by all the children in the class.
	The book is being read by Roda at the moment.
They finished the exam on time.	
	The mistakes were noticed by the maths teacher.

Focus on vocabulary

Compound nouns

11 The following compound nouns are in the text on internet shopping on page 50. Can you find them?

laptops   websites   online

Remember, a compound noun is a noun made up of two or more words.

The words on their own have a meaning but when they are joined they make a word with another meaning, for example:
a) lap + top = laptop
b) course + book = coursebook
c) check + out = check-out.

A compound noun can be a combination of any of the following:
- Noun + noun, e.g. web + site = website
- Adjective + noun, e.g. super + market = supermarket
- Verb + noun, e.g. walking + stick = walking stick
- Preposition + noun, e.g. on + line = online
- Noun + verb, e.g. hair + cut = haircut
- Noun + preposition, e.g. dressing + up = dressing up

12 Match the following words to create a compound noun.

Word 1	Word 2	Compound noun
police	head	
dining	cut	
water	by	
rain	put	
hair	man	
train	put	
passer	ware	
hanger	speaking	
driving	looker	
swimming	stander	
green	pool	
soft	fall	
red	spotting	
out	tank	
dry	house	
public	throw	
on	licence	
by	on	
over	cleaning	
in	table	

E Let's write

Facts and opinions

A fact is something that can be proven to be true. An opinion is a point of view or belief.

1 Which of these two sentences is fact and which is opinion? Why?

Cats are lovely animals.

Cats have good eyesight at night.

2 Find an example of a factual statement and an opinion in the passage from 'Let's read 1' on page 47.

Explain why you chose them.

3 What sort of texts are mainly factual and what sort are mainly opinions?

With your partner, find **five** more examples of text for each type and give reasons why.

Fact	Opinion
a) <u>Official reports</u> because there would be statistics to back up the material and it would be based on surveys.	

4 Now think of **six** more facts about money and **six** opinions about money. This time work on your own.

Fact	Opinion
a) Money is used in most countries of the world.	

5 Write a report about money using the seven facts from Exercise 4, but also add some opinion. Read the text to your friend and ask them to tell you the seven pieces of factual information that you have used, and which parts were opinion.

F Let's do some research

You are going to do some research about the economy of your country, or the economy of another country. When you have collected all the information, you will make a presentation to your class.

Here are some areas to include in your presentation:
- a brief history of its currency and how and when it was acquired
- the GDP of your country compared to other countries
- the extent to which it is a cash society
- how much it has been affected by globalisation
- what major investments there are in the economy
- what the rate of inflation is
- the use of e-banking
- how consumerist your society is, and why/why not.

G Let's learn something new

- The smell left on your hands after touching coins is from the human body. It is skin oils which are affected by the metal in the coins!
- On average, a US one-dollar note lasts for about 18 months and a coin lasts for about 25 years.
- There are 191 official currencies worldwide.

Unit 5 Our political world

A Let's start

1 Look at the two maps below and with your partner talk about the following:

- How are they different?
- Which one would you see from space?
- Who decides where the lines of a political map are drawn?
- How important can it be to people where borders of countries are?
- Why do the borders of countries change?
- How might the political map be different if it were the year 1900?
- Name three main events which might have changed borders.

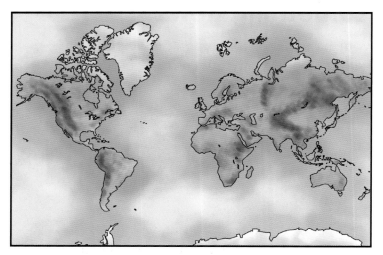

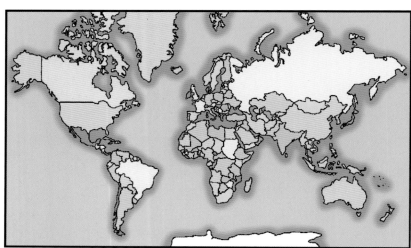

2 Do you know who these people are? Why are they famous? Do you know the names of any other famous national/international politicians?

3 Here are the names of some more famous political leaders. Match their names, and the politicians from Exercise 2, with the information below.

George Washington   Fidel Castro
Margaret Thatcher   Angela Merkel
Mustafa Kemal Ataturk   Mao Tse Tung
Mikhail Gorbachev   Jacques Chirac

- She was one of the first female leaders in Europe.
- He was a former president of South Africa and is now a peace activist.
- He was the first president of the United States.
- He was the founder of his country as a Republic and modernised the constitution.
- He was a revolutionary leader who governed for about 49 years.
- He was the last head of the USSR and helped bring about the end of the Cold War.
- He was a major political and spiritual leader after independence.
- She was the first German female Chancellor.
- A 'little red book' was published with his quotes and he led the Communist party in his country.
- A very popular President and second-longest serving one in his country.

4 With your partner, think of four other national or international political leaders and write a sentence to describe each of them. Read your sentences to the rest of the class and see if they can guess who the politicians are.

5 You are now going to look at some vocabulary that is connected to the world of politics – we have already used some in Exercise 3. Can you guess what the words are which are being described below?

- This is a country that is not led by a king or queen.
- This is a system of government where the rules and laws are often written.
- This is a system of government that promotes equality and common ownership.
- This is a title which refers to the leader of a country or business.

6 Now look at these other words and match them to the explanations below.

Parliament	Cabinet	Right-wing	Veto
Election	Democracy	Opposition	Minister
Member of	Dictator	Upper house	Legislation
Parliament	Left-wing	Monarchy	
(MP)			

- a person with total and absolute power
- a system with a king and/or queen
- those who stand against the government
- the law of the country
- a system where the government is chosen by the people
- a body of high-ranking members of a government, typically the executive
- a person who is an elected member of his/her government
- a decision-making process where a government is chosen to represent the people
- the position held in politics that supports a more equal society
- where policies and laws of the executive authority of the government can be questioned
- the system in politics that supports the more traditional authorities of power
- where a party can stop a certain piece of legislation
- the place where a country's government and opposition partywork
- member of the government who is chosen to deal with one aspect, e.g. defence, education, etc.

B Let's read 1

1 How much do you and your classmates know about the system of government in your country? In groups, answer the questions below.

a) What is the name of your current leader?
b) What system of government do you have in your country?
c) What is the party in power at the moment?
d) How long does a government normally stay in power?
e) How long does a leader normally stay in power?
f) Who has voting rights in your country?
g) What is the name of your parliament?
h) What are some of the main features of your parliament?
i) How long has the present political system existed in your country?
j) What system existed before?
k) What is the main party in opposition at the moment?
l) Who is its leader?
m) When were the last elections held?
n) What percentage of MPs are women?

2 During a war or conflict, the system of government often changes. This was true in the United Kingdom during World Wars I and II. A very popular Prime Minister during World War II was the man in the photo. How much do you know about him? Find out by matching the questions on the left to the answers on the right.

What was his name? Where was he from? Which country was he leader of? Which political party was he a member of? Why is he famous? Was he a good leader? How long did he lead the country for? What period in history was he leader for? What was one of the worst things he did? What was one of the best things he did?	For his supportive war-time speeches and bringing the UK victorious out of the war. Winston Churchill. Ended the war with the UK on the winning side. Yes, and very popular. From 1940–45 and 1951–55. United Kingdom. Oxfordshire, England. World War II. Return to the Gold standard where coins were again made in gold. The Liberal and Conservative parties.

3 But what makes a politician a good or a bad one? With your partner, talk about the following:

- Apart from Winston Churchill, what other good politicians can you think of?
- Why do you think they are good politicians?
- What characteristics do you think make a good politician?
- What characteristics do you think make a bad politician?
- Who do you think makes the best politician – a man or a woman? Why?
- Apart from the two mentioned in this unit, do you know of any other female politicians?
- Do you think it matters if a politician is male or female? Why?
- How do you think your country would vote if they were asked:

  'Who do you think makes the best politician – a man or a woman?'

4 You are now going to read an article about female politicians, but before you do that, how do you think the following regions and countries would feel about the issue? Talk about it with your partner and then quickly read the passage to see if you were correct.

| North America | Latin America | Kuwait |
| Western Europe | Russia | Bangladesh |

How the world rates women as leaders

In 2007 Cristina Fernandez de Kirchner was inaugurated as Argentina's first female president. She will join 11 other women who currently serve as their country's presidents or prime ministers. But while women worldwide are making gains in all levels of government, most people around the world express mixed opinions about women and political leadership.

The countries of Western Europe, North America and Latin America generally include the highest proportion of respondents who rate men and women as equally good political leaders. Roughly two-thirds in Kirchner's country (68%) express the view, while 17% say men are better leaders and 9% prefer women. In the United States, fully three-quarters say men and women make equally good political leaders, and that opinion is even more widespread in Western Europe.

By contrast, majorities in Mali (65%), the Palestinian territories (64%), Kuwait (62%), Pakistan (54%), Bangladesh (52%) and Ethiopia (51%) say men make better political leaders than women, as do nearly half of Jordanians (49%) and Nigerians (48%). Russians are also divided: 44% say men and women make equally good leaders while 40% say men are better.

Opinions about women in political leadership positions are connected with the extent to which women hold leadership roles in that country. These countries receive the highest score and are generally more likely to say that men and women make equally good political leaders. For example, in Sweden, the highest-ranking country in terms of female political empowerment, fully nine in ten say men and women are equally good leaders. In Kuwait, on the other hand, where women were given the right to vote and to run for office for the first time in 2005, only one third say men and women are equally good as political leaders, while more than six in ten (62%) say men are better.

5 Say if the following are true, false, or if the information is not given.
  a) Cristina Fernandez de Kirchner was Latin America's first female president.
  b) There are 11 other women who serve in government with her.
  c) Western Europe and the Americas rate the highest in thinking that men and women make equally good leaders.
  d) In Argentina 17 per cent of men and 9 per cent of women replied to the survey.
  e) More people in Western Europe than in North America think that men and women would be equally good political leaders.
  f) Russia has the lowest figures in all the countries surveyed.
  g) The statistics have a lot to do with a woman's role in the society asked.
  h) Sweden would come out top in all the countries asked.
  i) People first started to vote in Kuwait in 2005.
  j) One third of women are political leaders in Kuwait.

C Let's speak and listen

1 You are going to set up your own political party. To do this you need to follow these stages:
  ● Choose the members of your party – how?
  ● Choose the leader – how?
  ● Decide on a name for the party – how?
  ● Decide on a logo for the party – how?
  ● Decide on the policies of the party – how?

Once you have done this you are going to prepare your election campaign. You need to convince as many members of your class as possible to vote for you. The party that receives the most votes will be the winners of the election.

Your teacher and other members of your class will complete a copy of the following while each party is making their presentation. Give each party marks from 1–10, with 10 being the highest.

	Marks (1–10)
How effective is the name of the party?	
How effective is the logo?	
How effective is the leader? • How clearly do they speak? • Do they look you in the eye when they speak? • How clearly do they pronounce the language? • Do they stand and talk, and use their body to speak? • Do you feel that they believe in what they are saying? • Do you feel they are well prepared or do they just read their notes? • Do you feel they are speaking and listening to you? • Is there humour and jokes in the speech? • Was the speech too long, too short or just right?	
What were their policies?	
Choice of policies to get votes	
List the main policies: a) b) c)	

2 Now you are going to listen to another student who has taken part in the presentation. Complete, as far as possible, another copy of the chart above with details of their speech.

D Let's read 2

1 With your partner, talk about the following and choose from the possible answers.

Question	Possible answers
1 How interested would you say young people are in politics?	20% 40% 50% 70% 90% 100%
2 At what age do you think young people should be able to vote?	14 16 18 21
3 At what age do you think young people should be allowed to drive?	14 16 18 21 25

Question	Possible answers
4 At what age do you think children should be held responsible for criminal acts?	8 10 12 14 16 18 21
5 At what age do you think children should be allowed to work?	11 12 13 14 15 16
6 At what age do you think children should be able to leave school?	11 12 13 14 15 16
7 When do you think a young person should be seen as a fully-fledged adult?	14 16 18 21 25

2 Now look at the following age-related statistics for the UK and compare them with those in your country and the answers you gave in Exercise 1.

Issue	Age in the United Kingdom	Your country
Criminal responsibility	8	
Part-time work	13	
Leave school	16	
Full-time work	16	
Buy cigarettes	18	
Pay tax	16	
Join the army	16	
Leave home	16	
Get married	16	
Drive a car	17	
Vote	18	
Be a fully-fledged adult	21	

3 You are now going to read a passage about teenagers and voting.

Teenagers in the world of politics

They're old enough to join the army, so why can't 16-year-olds vote? Because they're not interested?

The mention of politics is a surefire way to make teenagers fall asleep. Ask them if they think the country's leader is doing a good job and they'll probably just nod and smile, completely uninterested. But ask them if they agree with being taxed at 16, or if they think they should have more rights – to drive, for example – and they could go on for hours. But surely that's politics, too?

We are deemed responsible enough to join the army and to make a decision about our education that will affect us for the rest of our life, so why are we not mature enough to make decisions about the country that we live in? Matters of schools and education apply to young people more than anyone else – it is our education, after all, that is affected by changes in funding or policy. Is it fair that these decisions are made by balding 40-somethings whose worst memories of school are taking exams? Do they know what it's like to sit a GCSE? Do they know what it's like to have leaking corridors and one computer between three students? I doubt it. So surely the people most knowledgeable in this area are us, the teenagers?

Perhaps voting in elections is too big a deal to be trusted to 16-year-olds, but we should be able to voice our views and vote on the issues that affect us.

If the government gives us the vote, we wouldn't try to take over the world, or vote for the water system to be replaced with Sprite. We would just like to have our say, like everyone else.

Focus on grammar

Infinitives

4 Here are some examples of the infinitive form used in the passage about teenagers in the world of politics:

| to make | to join | to have | to drive |

The infinitive form is simple to recognise because it consists of the word 'to' plus a verb in its simplest form.

We use this form for the following. Match the use with the example sentence.

Use	Example
a) To express purpose b) After certain verbs, e.g. • forget, help, learn, teach, train • choose, expect, hope, need, offer, want, would like • agree, encourage, pretend, promise, recommend • allow, can/can't afford, decide, manage, mean, refuse c) After certain adjectives, e.g. happy, glad, sorry, afraid, disappointed, pleased, relieved, sad, surprised d) After *too/enough* constructions e) To express specific preference with: I would like / would love / would prefer	i) They are too young to join the army. ii) They would prefer to wait until tomorrow. iii) He studied hard to become the best in his class. iv) They're glad to be here again. v) He agreed to bring the money tomorrow.

Some verbs can take the infinitive or the -ing form as long as the meaning of the verb does not change. Look at these examples:

It continued to rain all day.   or   It continued raining all day.

They like to go to the zoo.   or   They like going to the zoo.

The meaning has remained the same.

But with other verbs the meaning of the sentence changes.
For example:

Heinrich stopped to ask for directions.   =   He stopped the car and
                                                                asked somebody the way.

Heinrich stopped asking for directions.   =   He doesn't ask people
                                                                for directions any more.

5 Look at the following sentences and decide which form of the verb given in square brackets should be used: the infinitive, -ing, or both.
  a) He decided _____ for the whole year. [pay]
  b) The children liked _____ down the hill. [roll]
  c) He wanted _____ down his sleeves as he felt cold. [roll]
  d) They like _____ on time as they are punctual people. [arrive]
  e) They should be _____ soon as their plane has just landed. [arrive]
  f) The children love _____ to the beach at the weekends. [go]
  g) They like _____ to the cinema with their friends. [go]
  h) You need _____ at his homework when he has finished it. [look]
  i) Just _____ at it is no good; you need to read it as well. [look]
  j) The little girl started _____ when she was left at school. [cry]
  k) The children were _____ because the teacher had got angry with them. [cry]
  l) She forgot _____ the books back to the library. [take]
  m) She was asked _____ the books to the class. [take]
  n) The teacher regretted _____ the children that they would not be going. [tell]
  o) They were asked the things on the desk. [leave]

Focus on vocabulary

Apostrophes

6 Find nine examples of apostrophes used in the passage on pages 63–64.

7 Match the examples from the passage with each of the following:
- a shortened form of a word
- five examples of where two words are made into one
- possession.

Apostrophes are used in speech and informal writing. Apostrophes to show shortened forms of words are not usually used in formal writing.

It is easy to get confused with the use of apostrophes. This is because the words often sound the same, but when they are written, the meaning is different. For example:

They're (they are) late again *NOT* Their late again.

We're (we are) coming later *NOT* Were coming later.

You're (you are) very naughty *NOT* Your very naughty.

Apostrophes are used in the following ways:
- To show a shortened form of a word, e.g. can't = cannot.
- To join words together, e.g. they're = they are.
- To show possession in single nouns, e.g. the boy's book.
- To show possession in plural forms that don't end in 's', e.g. the children's toys.
- To show possession in plural forms that end in 's', e.g. the wives' dinner.
- Joint possession, e.g. Sara and George's wedding.
- In compound nouns, e.g. My sister-in-law's birthday.
- In time, e.g. nine o'clock (o' = of the).

8 Rewrite the following with apostrophes where necessary.
   a) They have decided not to come today.
   b) It has been decided that they will pay the full amount.
   c) Its theirs not yours, so leave it alone.
   d) Thats its bowl, the one with the cat food.
   e) They are here so you had better go and welcome them.
   f) We have been invited to visit their home in Washington.
   g) He would be better if he slept longer.
   h) They are not very good at tidying up, are they?
   i) Those are my brothers and my brother-in-laws photographs.
   j) The hotels knives are made of silver.

E Let's write

The writer's audience

1 With a partner, answer the following questions about the passage on pages 63–64.
   - How old is the writer?
   - Why (give an example)?
   - What age group is he/she writing for?
   - Why (give an example)?
   - Where might you find this passage?
   - Why?
   - What purpose has the text been written for?
   - How effectively do you think the writer has written to his/her chosen audience?
   - Why?
   - How formal/informal is the passage? Give examples to support your answer.

2 Write down words/expressions from the text that you feel show how the writer is writing for the audience that you have talked about.

3 You are now going to write your own passage of about 250 words, using some of the words and expressions that you have found.

The title of your passage is:

Younger politicians make better politicians

F Let's do some research

1 In Section B, Exercise 2, we looked at a famous politician from the United Kingdom – Winston Churchill.

You are going to choose a politician of either national or international standing and do some research about them. You can do the research with a friend or by yourself. Look at the information that was given in the exercise and include this and other information in your research. Present your research with pictures and text.

G Let's learn something new

- King Henry VIII of England (1491–1597) had two of his wives' heads chopped off!
- The bomb that was dropped on Hiroshima, Japan in World War II killed about 140,000 people. And the name of the bomb? Little Boy!
- The Greek ruler Alexander the Great (336–323 BC) did not allow his soldiers to grow beards because he thought they could be grabbed by the enemy in a fight.

Unit 6 | World poverty

A Let's start

1 Look at the products listed below and, with your partner, decide which ones you would **need** to survive every day and which you would **want** to survive every day. Copy and complete a table like the one below.

Three balanced meals a day   Shoes
Telephone   New clothes
Medicine   Television
Electricity   A home
One basic meal a day   Money
Toiletries   Clean drinking water
Water for general use   Transport

Need	Want

2 Now with your partner, talk about the products in the **need** column and put them in order of priority, with the most important for survival coming first.

Looking at your **need** column, at what point would you say poverty exists? Give reasons for your answer.

3 Look at the following quotations about poverty and with your partner, talk about and note:
  a) what each one means to you
  b) how much you agree/don't agree with it and why.

Use a table like the one below to help organise your notes.

Quotations	What it means to you	Agree? Because …
'There is no wealth like knowledge, and no poverty like ignorance.' Gautama Buddha – philosopher		
'The mother of revolution and crime is poverty.' Aristotle – Ancient Greek philosopher		

Quotations	What it means to you	Agree? Because ...
'To have nothing is not poverty.' Latin proverb		
'In wealth many friends, in poverty not even relatives.' Japanese proverb		
'The most terrible poverty is loneliness, and the feeling of being unloved.' Mother Teresa of Culcutta		
'The inevitable consequence of poverty is dependence.' Samuel Johnson – English poet		

4 After thinking about the quotations that you have just read and talked about, have any of your ideas in Exercise 2 changed?

5 We have looked at different ideas about poverty, but why do you think some countries are so poor and others are not? What is it that makes a country poor or wealthy? With your partner, copy the table below and list five things that you think make a country wealthy and five things that make a country poor.

What makes a country wealthy?	What makes a country poor?
e.g. Natural resources	e.g. Extreme climate

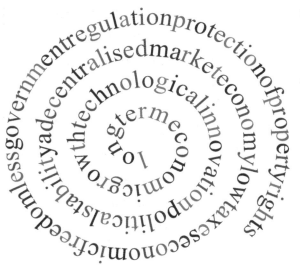

6 In the word circle on the left there are 10 other causes of poverty or wealth. Find them and put them in the correct categories in your table.

7 Match the words/expressions in the word circle with their definitions:
- Where a government is not free to take land that is owned privately by a person.
- Small rises in the price of goods.
- Where a country has a continual increase in what it produces, how much it trades, etc.
- Money charged by a government.
- Few government controls.
- The freedom to develop and research new ideas and practices.
- Where money is put into a company or business to improve it and make a gain.
- Where people have confidence in the political system because it is long-standing and established.

- When people are not controlled by the government on how they use their money.
- Where the government does not control how money is spent in the country.

B Let's read 1

We are going to look at some information about a country which is considered one of the poorest in the world. We will then compare it to one of the world's richest countries.

1 Look at the following information. Copy and complete the details on the right below. The first one has been done for you.

Freetown	71 740 sq km
Atlantic Ocean	Decade of civil war ended in 2002
41 years (men), 44 (women)	~~Republic of Sierra Leone~~
Leone	English, Krio (Creole)
–0.7%	Diamonds, rutile (mineral), cocoa,
West Africa	coffee, fish
US $220	Presidential elections
5.9 million	Islam, Christianity

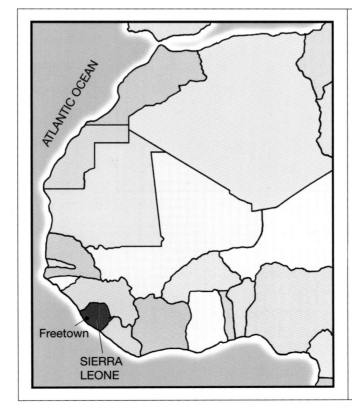

Official name of country:
Republic of Sierra Leone

Location in Africa:

Nearest sea/ocean:

Population:

Capital:

Area:

Main languages:

Main religions:

Life expectancy:

Currency:

Main exports:

GDP:

Yearly growth of economy:

Recent history:

Political system:

2 Now do the same for this country:

North central Europe	5.1%
Christianity	French, German, Luxembourgish
Founder member of the	Euro
European Economic Community	US $65 630
2586 sq km	Belgium, France and Germany
Grand Duchy of Luxembourg	Parliamentary representative
467 000	democracy
Steel products, chemicals, rubber	76 years (men), 82 years
products	(women)
Luxembourg	

Official name of country:

Location in Europe:

Neighbouring countries:

Population:

Capital:

Area:

Main languages:

Main religion:

Life expectancy:

Currency:

Main exports:

GDP:

Yearly growth of economy:

Recent history:

Political system:

3 With your partner, look at the statistics of the two countries and compare them. Look specifically at the areas listed below that we have already covered in this unit. Comment on how they would help or hinder a country's development.
- Long-term economic growth
- Political stability
- Life expectancy
- Recent history
- Location in the world
- Exports
- GDP

4 You are now going to read the personal story of a woman from Sierra Leone who is working with the charity Save the Children.

SIERRA LEONE: the toughest place in the world to be born

In Sierra Leone one in four children won't make it to their fifth birthday.

Years of fighting have left the country with insufficient hospitals, clinics or trained doctors and nurses. So since 2005, we've (Save the Children) been working with the government to rebuild its healthcare system, ensuring that the poorest and most remote communities can get the essential healthcare they need.

Children whose homes are surrounded by dirty water face the constant threat of diarrhoea and cholera.

Recently, we've expanded our work into the slums of the country's capital, Freetown. We're training women like Adia to be a Blue Flag volunteer. They hang a blue flag outside their home to show they're qualified to treat diarrhoea – a disease that still kills more than a million children every year through malnutrition and dehydration.

"We live in the community so people have close access to us," says Adia. "Before, at night, people had nowhere to go for treatment. Now people can come and knock on our door at any time. They can be treated immediately, before they get even more sick."

Adia is clearly proud of her new role, saying, "It makes me feel happy to save a life in the community." This joy is shared by Adama, whose three-year-old son Mohammed was treated by Adia when he developed severe diarrhoea.

"Mohammed got sick when our home flooded this year," explains Adama. "I knew it was diarrhoea. It happened at a weekend, so the clinic was closed. But I took him to a Blue Flag volunteer who gave him oral rehydration salts. I knew where to find her because of the flag flying outside her home."

She adds, "My second child Mary got sick last year, before the Blue Flag volunteers were trained. By the time she was taken to the hospital she was very bad ... it's good having the Blue Flag volunteers in the community because we don't have to go so far to get treatment and we don't have to pay."

---

5 Find the following information in the passage above:
   a) two illnesses due to dirty water
   b) the reason why there are few trained nurses and doctors
   c) the percentage of children who won't live after their fifth birthdays
   d) the name of the charity
   e) the name of the campaign

f) two effects of diarrhoea which kill children

g) the name of the two women in the passage

h) the name of the two children mentioned in the passage

i) why Mohammed couldn't go to the clinic

j) what is given to a child when they have diarrhoea.

C Let's speak and listen

1 With your partner, talk about and find out what **you think** are the five wealthiest and five poorest countries in the world.

Then, for each country, think of at least one reason why they are either poor or wealthy.

Set out the information in a table like the one below.

Poor countries	Reasons for the poverty
e.g. Sierra Leone a) b) c) d) e)	• Has recently been involved in a civil war.
Wealthy countries	**Reasons for wealth**
e.g. Luxembourg a) b) c) d) e)	• Has a stable economy and government.

2 Look at the countries listed below. How many of them are the same as the countries you chose above?

3 Copy and complete the table opposite with the information that is missing, putting what you think is the wealthiest first and the poorest last (the figures below are in US dollars). Also, put the geographical location of each country by listing neighbouring countries, if you know any.

Austria	United States	Somalia
Ireland	$600	$800
$47 800	$35 500	Norway

$600   Malawi   East Timor
Yemen $43 500 $800
$43 600 $49 700 $900
Afghanistan   United Arab Emirates

Rank	Country	GDP per capita	Neighbouring countries
1			
2			
3			
4			
5			
6			
7			
8			
9			
10			

4 Now listen to the dialogue and see if your ideas were correct. Put the information in the correct place according to the dialogue, checking that you also have the geographical position of each country correct.

D Let's read 2

1 Look at the labels of the following items that you are wearing or have at school with you today. Where was each of them made?
- Your school bag
- Your pencil case
- Your shoes
- Your school shirt/blouse
- Your school skirt/trousers

Have you ever thought about how the clothes and school items came to be in your shops? Why are they so cheap? Who makes them? What are the ages of the people who make them?

2 Look at the following statistics:
- 284 000 West African children work on cocoa farms.
- Many cocoa farmers live in poverty.
- 61 per cent of working children live in Asia.
- In India, 32 million children don't go to school because they have to work.
- In Delhi, India, 1000 children recently protested because they want to go to school.

3 Look at these labels. Have you ever seen them before? Do you know what they are?

Because of the statistics above, there has recently been a movement called 'Fair Trade', which aims to pay more to the people who produce the items that are sent to the wealthy western world. The idea is to make people think more about what they are buying and who they are buying from, in order to try and reduce poverty.

4 Are there any other ways that you or your friends could reduce poverty in the world? Talk about it with your partner and list **five** ideas – one has been given for you.

Five ways I think poverty could be reduced in the world
1 Think about what I am buying and look for Fair Trade labels on products.
2
3
4
5

5 You are now going to read a passage about Fair Trade.

"Before you've finished your breakfast this morning, you'll have relied on half the world."
Martin Luther King

An interesting thought. And a depressing one, when you realise that those people you've relied on for your coffee and cereal are almost certainly being exploited and oppressed by the unfair balance in world trade.

But what can you do? Surely it's beyond your control? You can buy Fair Trade products.

Fair Trade is a growing, international movement which ensures that producers in poor countries get a fair deal. This means a fair price for their goods (one that gives them enough money to live on), security in their jobs and the opportunity to develop their businesses and increase sales.

This can only be achieved by changing the unfair rules of world trade so that they work for small-scale producers as well as rich multi-nationals.

In the meantime, for hundreds of thousands of people, Fair Trade means the difference between a hand-to-mouth existence, and being able to plan for the future.

In the past decade, the Fair Trade movement has really taken off – as consumer awareness of and indignation about the treatment of producers in poor countries has increased. More retailers than ever are stocking Fair Trade goods, the number of products on offer continues to grow as demand increases, and more poor communities are feeling the benefits.

Focus on grammar

Adjectives

An adjective describes the noun or pronoun to make it more interesting, e.g.

> the <u>tall</u> man
> the <u>delicious</u> cake

6 Find ten adjectives in the passage above. List them in your book.

7 Adjectives can often be recognised by how the word ends. Copy the examples below and then add two more of your own to each one:

Adjective ending	Example	Your examples
-able/-ible	comparable/intelligible	
-ful	wonderful	
-ous	wondrous	
-ive	attractive	
-ic	domestic	
-less	careless	
-al	intellectual	

Many, however, have no distinct form and can't be recognised. Here are some examples:

good / bad / dark / cold / simple / wicked / great / clever / silent

Adjectives can be used to compare two or more things, e.g.

The more wicked the witch, the cleverer you must be.

The most silent person could also be the cleverest.

8 Make sentences of your own using the following adjectives in any way you want:
a) wonderful, lucky
b) beautiful, poor
c) disastrous, embarrassing
d) poorest, amazing
e) funny, curious
f) terrifying, confusing.

If you use more than one adjective for description, then there is a certain order that needs to be followed. However, it is rare to use more than three adjectives together.

A beautiful, tall, young, thin, dark, African woman walked into the room.

1	2	3	4	5	6	7
Feeling	Size	Age	Shape	Colour	Origin	Material
beautiful	**tall**	**young**	**thin**	**dark**	**African**	**woman**

It would more usual to say:

> A beautiful, tall, African woman walked into the room. She was young, thin and dark ...

9 Now describe each of the following using the order 1–7 above:
- **a)** a car
- **b)** your best friend
- **c)** a beautiful object you like
- **d)** an ugly object you don't like.

Focus on vocabulary

Prefixes and suffixes

These are used in the formation of longer words from the root word.
- Prefixes go at the *beginning* of a word,
  e.g. in + complete = incomplete.
- Suffixes go at the *end* of a word, e.g. like + able = likeable.

10 Find two examples of a prefix and two examples of a suffix in the passage on page 77.

11 We will look at some common prefixes and suffixes and their meanings. Add your own examples in your copy of the table.

Prefix	Meaning	Example	Your example
anti-	against	antibacterial	
auto-	self	autobiography	
com-	with, together	community	
con-	with, together	connect	
dis-	not, apart	disappear	
il-	not	illegal	
im-	not	impossible	
micro-	small	microphone	
mono-	only	monopoly	
pre-	before	predict	
pro-	for, forward	project	
sub-	under	submarine	
tele-	far off	telephone	

Suffix	Meaning	Example	Your example
-cide	to kill	herbicide	
-ia, -y	act, state	mania, democracy	
-logy	study of	biology	
-ist	the person	biologist	
-oid	the shape of	spheroid	

E Let's write

Writing to inform

In the passage on page 77, the writer is telling us about Fair Trade and why we should support it. The writer knows that the reader does not know much about the subject. One way to help you understand is to write **clearly and effectively**.

1 Find an example of clear and effective language in the Fair Trade passage.

2 It is also important that **some facts** are given. Find two examples of facts in the passage.

3 Also, the passage should be written **logically and with structure**. Explain how the writer has done this in the text.

4 The writer does not use unnecessary language but **goes straight to the point**. Explain in your own words how the writer does this.

Where would you find this sort of writing? In the wordsearch on the next page, find seven places where you may find it and then suggest three more ideas of your own. One has been done for you.

```
A L F A S T F S E L O O K B A
K G U I D E B O O K S A A D C
S R P S W B A R T M N W V I R
E E A T F D R E K P F E O O S
T P G U B T Y H U L R B F R W
O O E A N R D K T T L P K G T
O R R R M A S J I Y V A B D C
A T T T S L K S T S G O O L
R S K O O B E C N E R E F E R
T K G D A M S E R T I S M N T
L N R L E A F L E T S K S R E
F O T N M H K S E L F A E L S
H K T D A D E V R T I M T S A
N S O S P Q R A̶R̶T̶I̶C̶L̶E̶S̶
```

F Let's do some research

With your partner, find out more about Fair Trade and design a web page using language to inform.

G Let's learn something new

- According to UNICEF 26 500–30 000 children die each day due to poverty.
- Nearly 1 billion people today can't read or sign their names.
- Some 1.8 million children die each year as a result of diarrhoea.

The weather

A Let's start

1 Look at the different pictures. Where do you think each one is?
Match the pictures to the locations given.

Locations:

Australasia

Middle East

Caribbean

Antarctica

North East Europe

Central Africa

2 Now look at the six descriptions and match each one to its location.

a) This region looks very green. It has high levels of precipitation, chilly winters and warm summers.	**b)** It is mostly a tropical area with warm weather conditions. Experiences very high humidity and hurricanes are a common feature of this area.	**c)** Large desert areas with very little precipitation. High temperatures and high levels of humidity along the coast.
d) This is the coldest place on Earth and can be described as a frozen desert. Throughout the year it remains under a thick sheet of snow.	**e)** There are seven different climatic zones because of the size of the continent. The weather for the region depends on the zone – whether tropical, savannah, equatorial, etc.	**f)** This region is situated in the southern hemisphere and experiences very diverse weather conditions, including extremely hot and dry summers.

3 How many words in the column on the left can you find in this unit so far? Now match the word to its definition given below. Write each word with its correct definition.

Word	Definition
Precipitation	a) The change in the pressure of the air
Tropical	b) To predict what something is to be
Humidity	c) Temperature scale where freezing point is 32°
Hurricane	d) A scientist who studies the weather
Desert	e) A temperature scale where the boiling point of water is 100°
Seasons	f) These regions are dominated by the Arctic and Antarctic
Savannah	g) Rainfall
Equator	h) An imaginary line that divides Earth into the Northern and Southern hemispheres
Highs and lows	i) Weather that is warm-to-hot and moist all year round
Celsius	j) Without extremes of weather
Fahrenheit	k) A wooded eco-system where trees stand sparsely
Meteorologist	l) The scenery or geography of a place
Landscape	m) The increase in the average temperature of the Earth
Greenhouse effect	n) The amount of water vapour in the air
Global warming	o) A storm system that brings strong winds and flooding rains
Temperate	p) A landscape that receives very little precipitation
Polar	q) Spring, Summer, Autumn (Fall) and Winter
Forecast	r) Energy captured by the atmosphere that is recycled

4 Use the words from the table on page 83 to complete this passage:

I have been travelling a lot in recent years and seen many different kinds of _____ but one that I really love because of the variety of flowers and fauna is the _____ one. It can be such a beautiful experience seeing the vast numbers of birds and plants in one small area. The problem of course is the level of _____ and the dangers of _____ in these areas, and you need to plan what time of year it is best to go. The levels of _____ can also be a problem and you can start off the day feeling nice and fresh, but then an hour later you're dripping again and wishing that you had taken a fresh change of clothes. Another area that has great fascination and charm is the _____ because although they are barren in comparison, they still have an immense beauty with their areas of vast emptiness and colours. The hottest I've ever been travelling through such a plain was at 45° _____ which I believe to be equivalent to 113° _____. A _____ friend of mine told me that those temperatures are not uncommon for that part of the world and that it is getting worse because of _____, and the _____ that all the world's industries and cars are having on the environment. So I wasn't so keen to go to the _____ regions again – you feel so exposed as there isn't much coverage during the middle of the day when the sun is pounding down on you.

The _____ regions are places that I have never been that interested in as I don't like feeling cold. I must admit to preferring the _____ climate, as each year I enjoy the experience of seeing the changes brought about by the _____, listening to the weather _____ and hearing what the _____ of pressure will bring us this week.

5 How much do you know about the weather? With your partner, look at the following and say if they are true or false.
   a) Libya (North Africa) is the hottest country in the world.
   b) Antarctica is the world's coldest place.
   c) The hottest temperature ever recorded is 57.8°C.
   d) Ethiopia has the highest average temperature in the world.
   e) The fastest wind ever recorded is 3717 kmph.
   f) The Atacama Desert (South America) is the driest place in the world.
   g) The coldest temperature ever recorded is minus 89.2°C.
   h) A rainbow is made up of six colours.
   i) Hail is frozen rain.
   j) The sound of thunder is made by rain falling.
   k) The safest place during a storm is under a tree.

l) An Indian Summer happens in the winter.

m) A barometer is used to measure air pressure.

n) Walking becomes difficult in winds of more than 22mph.

o) There is more oxygen in the atmosphere than any other gas.

B Let's read 1

1 With your partner, talk about and complete a copy of the table below.

- In column a, write the 12 months of the year.
- In column b, write why that month is special to you, e.g. your birthday, holidays.
- In column c, write words that you think of when you think of that month, e.g. warmth/lazy days, exams at school.

	a	b	c
1	January		
2	F		
3	M		
4			
5			
6			
7			
8			
9			
10			
11			
12			

2 Now read the poem on the next page and use the rhyme to help you decide where each of these words should go. To check your answers, ask your teacher.

showers	snow	pleasant
lambs	corn	feet
shoot	sleet	rain
fast	roses	daffodil

The Garden Year

January brings the (a)_____,
Makes our feet and fingers glow,
February brings the (b)_____,
Thaws the frozen lake again.
March brings breezes, loud and shrill,
To stir the dancing (c)_____.
April brings the primrose sweet,
Scatters daisies at our (d)_____.
May brings flocks of pretty (e)_____,
Skipping by their fleecy dams.
June brings tulips, lilies, (f)_____,
Fills the children's hands with posies.
Hot July brings cooling (g)_____,
Apricots, and gillyflowers.

August brings the sheaves of
(h)_____,
Then the harvest home is borne.
Warm September brings the fruit;
Sportsmen then begin to (i)_____.
Fresh October brings the pheasant;
Then to gather nuts is (j)_____.
Dull November brings the blast;
Then the leaves are whirling (k)_____.
Chill December brings the (l)_____,
Blazing fire, and Christmas treat.

Sara Coleridge

3 Do the following activities based on the poem.
   a) What sort of climate does the writer live in? Explain how you know this.
   b) What part of the world does the writer live in? How do you know this?
   c) Divide the poem into the seasons of the year.
   d) Choose four words that describe each of the seasons.
   e) Rewrite the poem using words and language you thought of with your friend in Exercise 1. Write two lines for each month and try to find words that rhyme, as in the poem.

 C # Let's speak and listen

The weather is more than just the sun and the rain that we see every day. As a result, many idioms in the English language have developed and become part of it, as have many stories which try to explain the scientific phenomenon.

The weather in the UK is very mixed and changeable. As a result, in the English language there are many idioms based on the weather and many stories which try to explain the science behind different weather events.

1 With your partner, talk about aspects of the weather and each of the weather events listed below, as in the example. Write one more with your own ideas at the end. Don't complete the last column yet.

Weather event	Story around it	What we see	Scientific explanation	Listening task
Rainbows	A pot of gold can be found at the end of the rainbow.	A beautiful arc of colours.	Light of the sun shining through drops of moisture.	
A gentle breeze				
A snow flake				
Thunder and lightning				
Hurricanes				
Fresh snow				
Icicles				
Clouds				
Other				

2 Now look at the different idioms that are connected to the weather and match them to their meaning.

Idiom	Meaning
1 To be on cloud nine.	a) Not realistic about things.
2 A fair weather friend.	b) Something will be easy.
3 To be as quick as lightning.	c) To overhear by mistake or hear gossip.
4 To take a rain check.	d) Very happy.
5 To be under the weather.	e) Whatever happens.
6 To get wind of something.	f) Do something at a later date.
7 Raining cats and dogs.	g) Not feeling well.
8 A ray of sunshine.	h) Something nice happens.
9 To have your head in the clouds.	i) Very fast.
10 A face like thunder.	j) Only friendly when it's easy.
11 A storm in a teacup.	k) Very heavy rain.
12 To be a breeze.	l) Very angry.
13 Come rain or shine.	m) A lot of fuss about nothing.

3 Now listen and check that you have:
   a) matched the correct idiom with its meaning
   b) completed the final column of the table in Exercise 1 by matching the idioms to the weather events.

D Let's read 2

1 Look at these newspaper headlines:

Heavy rain drenches Puerto Rico

Transatlantic flights delayed by freak weather

Typhoon hits China coast 100 000 evacuated

Two prize ponies killed by lightning as freak weather hits Britain

2 We can see that extreme weather can affect people's lives. With your partner, look at the following weather conditions and talk about what happens when these extremes of weather occur. Look at the example to help you. Think of more than one example for each category.

Rain	Snow	Ice	Wind	Desert storms	Sun
					Drought – farmers can't grow crops and animals die.

3 You will find ten examples of words connected to weather extremes in the word circle below. Find them and then use the words to complete the crossword opposite.

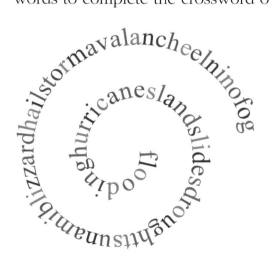

Crossword clues

1. Heavy rain results in land moving because any natural support, e.g. trees, have been removed.

2. A mixture of liquid and frozen precipitation that falls heavily, causing damage.

3. An unusually large ocean wave caused by an undersea earthquake or volcanic eruption.

4. Days of heavy rain and/or melting snow result in rivers rising and going over their banks.

5. A period where there is a lack of rainfall.

6. An intense winter storm with high winds and snow.

7. A cloud that is in contact with the ground and reduces visibility.

8. A large body of snow, ice or rock sliding down a mountain.

9. Unusual warming of surface waters in the South Pacific that can then influence global weather.

10. Intense storms with swirling winds.

4 You are now going to read a passage about snow – an extreme weather.
- Where is Denver, Colorado?
- What is important to some people about the date 24 December?
- What sort of weather would you expect to have at that time of year?

Adventures in Snow!

One of Colorado's most powerful blizzards, The Blizzard of 1982, covered the city of Denver with several feet of snow on December 24th, 1982.

I was 10 years old then, and delighted to be enjoying a winter break from school. We were doing the final round of shopping and preparations for the feast which was to take place on Christmas Eve. But no one could have expected the scene we awoke to that morning.

The snow had begun to fall on the evening of the 23rd. The snow fell very quickly and each hour another inch of snow fell, building up rapidly. By the morning of the 24th, our car was buried in the driveway and snow was piled up against the doors of the house. The wind was blowing snow into huge drifts that reached the second storey of the house. The power would go out for short periods of time and then come back on.

For my sisters and I, this was an adventure. For my parents, it was a bit of a nightmare. We had to get to the store, so we worked frantically to uncover the car and a path to the street. My mom and uncle carefully drove to the store, and were lucky enough to find a nearby market that was open.

As the amount of snow increased dramatically, us kids decided to dig a tunnel from the back door down a long walkway to the back of the yard. We were able to get the back door open just enough to sneak out and begin digging – first with our hands, then using garden tools. It took several hours to build this remarkable tunnel. My dad packed the snow firmly for us, to make sure that the tunnel wouldn't cave in on anyone.

The tunnel kept us busy for quite some time, but we couldn't resist another adventure – jumping off the roof into giant snowdrifts. My sisters and I crept out a second storey window onto the garage, and leapt into the huge 10-foot pile of snow on the side of the house. When my mom, who had been working in the kitchen, got word of this activity, she promptly steered us inside and gave us a major scolding.

For my family, the blizzard was not tragic. In fact, it gave us some amazing opportunities, but of course other people were not so lucky.

Focus on grammar

Past tenses

5 Find an example of each of the following from the passage above:
- The past simple as a regular verb and as an irregular verb.
- The past perfect.
- The past continuous.
- The past perfect continuous.

6 Match the use of the tenses to the examples given below.

Use	Example
a) Actions which happen one after the other.	i) I was watching TV as Mark was cooking the dinner.
b) Past habits.	ii) She had been smoking for 10 years before she stopped.
c) Action which happened at a definite time in the past.	iii) They left that house 10 years ago.
d) Action happening at a stated past time.	iv) They were going to the cinema when it started to rain.
e) Interrupted action in the past.	v) He was sick because he had eaten too much.
f) Actions happening at the same time.	vi) They had cooked the dinner before I got there.
g) Past action which happened before a stated past time.	vii) He took the saucepan, put in the milk and heated it up.
h) Past action connected to another past action.	viii) They were listening to the radio at 14.30 yesterday.
i) Action continuing up to a period of time in the past.	ix) He used to play football every Sunday.

7 Match each of the sentences below with one of the forms given in the left-hand column above.
   a) They had cleaned up before I got home.
   b) They ate a whole cake yesterday.
   c) They had no money because they had spent it all.
   d) They were swimming while I was sunbathing.
   e) I was eating my dinner at 6 o'clock yesterday!
   f) She had been trying to lose weight for five months before she lost anything.
   g) While I was working we had a power cut.
   h) I washed up, then I put the things in the cupboard and then sat down tired.
   i) He practised every day last year.

8 Correct the tense errors in the following sentences.
   a) I was walked down the road when I saw my best friend.
   b) He was taking off his shirt, having a shower and then going to bed.
   c) She was sleeping for ten hours before she got woken up.
   d) The film starting an hour ago.

e) She walks into school at 08.30 yesterday.

f) They were tired because they not sleeped last night.

g) They had wrote the wrong answer to the question.

h) The bucket leaked as he filled it up.

i) They had went to the best restaurant in town.

j) They had destroyed the garden by the time I get there.

Focus on vocabulary

American English

There are differences in spelling, meaning and grammatical usage between some British English (BE) and American English (AE) words. It is important to be consistent when you write – in other words, do not switch between BE usage and AE usage.

9 We know that the passage on page 90 is probably written by an American because it is based in Denver, Colorado, but also because there are certain words used that are typically American. What are they?

10 Read the following sentences and:
   a) say if they are American English (AE) or British English (BE)
   b) write down the word/s that show this
   c) rewrite the sentence so that it is in the other form of English.

   Use a dictionary to check if you are not sure.

- There was a huge accident as a truck drove up onto the sidewalk.
- The boy's pants were filthy as he had spilt paint all over them.
- The baby kept crying because he wanted his dummy and his nappy was wet.
- That boy got really mean with me when I ate the last cookie.
- The soccer players were wearing the new sweaters of their teams.
- The cinema was on fire and it was dangerous to use the lifts.
- I was running out of gas and there were no places to buy any on the highway.
- 'Excuse me, could you tell me where the bathroom is, please?'
- She is such a fussy eater and never wants a cookie or potato chips.
- The letter was posted when I was on holiday but it must have had the wrong postcode on the envelope.

 **Let's write**

Writing your own short story

You read a short story called 'Adventures in Snow!' in this unit. You are now going to write your own short story, but before you do that you need to think about some important features of writing a story.

1 Look at the following areas that should be included in a story and complete a copy of the table with answers about 'Adventures in Snow!'

	Plot and theme	Characters	Narrative	Setting
	What is the story going to be about? What is going to happen in the story?	Who are they?	Is it going to be written in the first/third person? Is it going to be formal/informal?	Where and when will the story be set?
'Adventures in the Snow!'				
Your story				

2 Before you begin to write your story, you will also need to think about the following:
  - Why is it important to plan before you begin to write?
  - What sort of information should you include in your plan?
  - Why is it important that you think about who you are writing for?
  - Why is it important that your story should be interesting?
  - How can you make your story interesting?
  - Why is it important to check your spelling, grammar, etc. when you have finished?

3 Now you are going to write your story.

The title of your story is:

Adventures in the _____.

F Let's do some research

What does each of the following mean? To what extent do you believe them? Think of some more from your own culture and translate them into English.

Red sky at night, sailor's delight!
Red sky in the morning, sailor's warning.

If there are lots of berries on the dogberry tree, it means it's going to be a bad winter.

If the leaves are turning up, a storm is brewing.

Sharks go out to sea at the approach of a wave of cold weather.

G Let's learn something new

- Sunbathing even on a cloudy day can be dangerous.
- A typical flash of lightning lasts about 0.2 seconds.
- At any particular time, there are approximately 1800 thunderstorms in the Earth's atmosphere.

Today's world adventurers

A Let's start

1 Imagine that you were going to travel round the world and there were two different routes you could choose from: either North to South or East to West.

Which countries would you see if you travelled North to South?

Which countries would you see if you travelled East to West?

Imagine that the starting and finishing point for both routes is **Turkey**. Copy the table below and put the following countries in the order you would see them.

Turkey	Arctic	Sudan	Russia
Antarctica	Ukraine	Alaska	Zambia
France	Egypt	United States	Japan
Afghanistan	Korea	of America	
China	South Africa	Iran	
Hawaii	Italy	Hungary	

North to South travel	East to West travel

2 Here are pictures of places you might see if you travelled around the world. Where are they? Why are they famous? Now think of six more famous places around the world. Tell your partner the names of the places and ask them in which country they would be found.

3 Use an atlas to check the countries you would travel through if you were to travel North to South and East to West from your country. List the countries in the order that you would travel through them. If you live in Turkey, choose a different country to start from.

Which countries would you like to travel through? Why?

Which countries would you not like to travel through? Why?

What would be the most exciting or challenging part of your journey? Why?

B Let's read 1

Imagine how different it is for adventurers today compared to adventurers in the past.

1 With your partner, talk and think about what adventurers in the past *didn't* have to complete their journeys compared to what they have today. Copy and complete the following table to help you.

Adventurers of the past	
Names of adventurers in the past	
What sort of people were they? e.g. education, etc.	
Countries/places they went to	
The methods used to explore, e.g. transportation	
The equipment they had to help them	
The reasons they went	
What they brought back from their travels	
Where they got financing from for their travels	

2 Now do the same with modern-day adventurers.

Adventurers today	
Type of adventurers today	
What sort of people are they? e.g. education, etc.	
Countries/places they go to	
The methods used to explore, e.g. transportation	
The equipment they have to help them, e.g. technology	
The reasons they go (and how are they different?)	
What they would bring back from their travels (Would it be the same kind of things, e.g. tobacco, potatoes, etc.?)	
Where they would get financing from for their travels (Would it be from kings or queens as in the past?)	

3 Bikes are a form of transport that have been around for more than 100 years and more recently they have been used as a method of transport for adventurers. But could bikes have been used by adventurers over 100 years ago? Why/why not? Think of at least **four** reasons to support your answer.

4 Look at the pictures of the two bikes and the cyclists and compare them. What has the second bike and cyclist got that the first one hasn't?

5 Imagine that you were going to cycle round the world. How many days do you think it would take today? Do not include any rest days, or days used for other necessary forms of transportation to cross sea, etc.

112 days and 8 hours / 195 days and 6 hours / 264 days and 11 hours

6 By cycling round the world you would come across many wonderful things but also many dangers. With your partner, talk about both the nice experiences you would have, but also some of the dangers and difficulties you might come across. Use your route to help you and think about the following areas:
- the seasonal weather
- language problems
- access to technology
- different cultures
- different authorities, e.g. police, immigration, etc.
- diet
- money
- safety.

7 Now read the passage below and find the answer to Exercise 5.

Briton fastest ever to cycle round the world

A Briton has become the fastest person ever to cycle round the world, peddling past the finishing line in Paris 195 days and six hours after he set out.

Tanned, bearded and flanked by a police escort, Mark Beaumont was greeted by cheers from family and friends at the end of an epic journey that has taken him through 20 countries.

He suffered water poisoning in Iran and food poisoning in Pakistan, and was knocked off his bike three times – by a donkey in Pakistan, a motorbike in India and in Florida by an old woman in a car.

Mugged in Louisiana, locked up by police in Pakistan, and nearly washed away by torrential rains in Thailand, Mr Beaumont, 25, said he "never felt like giving up".

He had to cycle 18 000 miles (28 968.1 km). Flying time was not counted but the stopwatch started ticking as soon as the bike had cleared customs.

He lost a stone (6.3 kg) in weight but he said he made some "amazing friendships" along the way, and had time to take in some amazing sights.

After initial saddle sores, his body got accustomed to the daily routine, but mentally there were tough moments. "There were long stretches where I didn't speak to anyone and had no contact. I took a lot of strength from the fact that a lot of people were watching a little dot on a GPS map and knew where I was," he said. His position was updated every two hours on his website via satellite.

On his travels he raised money for charities, one of which was Tusk, which supports wildlife. He has already raised around £5000 but expects to make at least another £10 000 now that he has crossed the finishing line. Mr Beaumont said he was not sure what to do next: "It's really a blank canvas now. You'll have to ask me that in a few days. I intend to sleep for about a fortnight."

8 Look at the points in Exercise 6 and find which ones came up in the passage.

Comment in your own words how each one is mentioned.

9 Complete the following sentences about the passage above.
   a) It took Mr Beaumont _____ to travel _____.
   b) He travelled across _____.
   c) He was _____ three times: _____ in Pakistan, _____ and _____.
   d) He travelled _____.
   e) He lost _____.

f) His family knew where he was by _____.

g) He collected _____ and hopes to _____.

h) He plans to _____.

C Let's speak and listen

A group of young adventurers have been asked to join a research team in Antarctica to research the homing habits of penguins for six months. There is one place left to complete the team and you have been asked to select the final candidate.

1 Before you look at the candidates, you need to think and talk about the sort of person who you think would be a suitable candidate.

With a partner, talk about the following and make notes for each one:
- their personal characteristics
- their fitness
- their background
- their interests/hobbies
- the reasons they want to go
- relevant experience.

2 Listen to the four candidates talking and complete the information about them in a copy of the table below.

	Candidate No 1	Candidate No 2	Candidate No 3	Candidate No 4
Person's name and personal details				
Their personal characteristics				
Their fitness				
Their background				
Their interests/hobbies				
The reasons they want to go				
Relevant experience				

3 Now that you have the information, talk to your partner about each one and decide who you think the best candidate would be. Your teacher will ask you who you choose, and you will need to support your decision.

D Let's read 2

The Arctic and the Antarctic
(the North Pole and the South Pole)

1 Talk to your partner about the following.
- What is the difference between the Arctic and the Antarctic?
- What is similar between the two?
- Why do so many adventurers want to go there?
- What do people research there?
- What do the North and South Poles have to offer?
- Why do so many people die there?
- Who do the North and South Poles belong to?
- Are they countries?

2 Look at the following facts and decide whether they describe the Artic or the Antarctic or both. Your teacher will help you.

The Arctic	The Arctic and the Antarctic	The Antarctic

Has 90% of the world's ice.
Covered in snow and ice.
Has tundra (low tree growth).
Nobody has ever lived there.
Has the coldest, driest, windiest weather in the world.
Sun never sets in the summer.
Has towns.
Has freezing temperatures of 250°C.
Has seals, whales and dolphins.
Rich plant life in the spring and summer.

Arid (severe lack of available water).
Is a continent.
Has many natural resources.
Has indigenous (ethnic) people.
Has no government and belongs to no country.
Science stations exist for research.
Has icebergs.
Has penguins.
Has polar bears.

3 Over the years, explorers and adventurers have been to the Arctic and the Antarctic. Talk about the following with your partner:

- What is it about these places that attracts people?
- What dangers are there that are different from the dangers we saw earlier in this unit?
- Would you like to go to the Arctic or the Antarctic? Why/why not?
- Do you know of any adventurers who have been? Did they succeed in their adventure?

4 You are now going to read about two adventurers who have been to both the Arctic and the Antarctic.

Belgians Alain Hubert and Dixie Dansercoer will step off the Siberian mainland and onto the frozen Arctic Ocean in an attempt to complete the longest-ever crossing of the Arctic basin.

Over the next 110 days, they will ski, stomp, and sail – aided by giant kites – to the southern tip of Greenland, more than 2500 miles (4020 km) away. In 1998, the pair completed a world record-setting 2438-mile (3924-km) Antarctica crossing, but this trek poses many different challenges.

Ten years ago you and Dixie Dansercoer set the record for the longest crossing of Antarctica by foot and ski. How will crossing the Arctic compare to crossing Antarctica?

Hubert: Much of the (Arctic) traverse will be on sea ice, which is always moving. It's impossible to know what will happen in the coming hours. But as soon as we get to the ice cap on Greenland we expect to sail (across the ice) quite a lot. You quite often get bad weather, but it's good because then you get the wind. Greenland is a paradise for kites because the snow is a bit soft. In Antarctica you have sastrugis – this is a Russian word with no translation. It's like an icy wave, as hard as concrete, which makes it impossible to sail.

This expedition has certain educational and scientific goals.

Hubert: Yes, as we are working for the European Space Agency, which is the equivalent of NASA in the US. Every 20 miles (30 km), we will take a measurement of the snow's thickness. But we are also sportsmen and would like to complete the longest crossing of the Arctic basin. And I think it's important to make people dream about the Poles because this planet is changing much faster than before. We need young people, new adventurers, new explorers, new scientists going to these areas much more.

Focus on grammar

Future tenses

5 Find two examples of the future tense in the passage opposite. Why is the future tense used here?

6 Match the following so you have nine sentences about the future tense.

a) We use *will* to express things …	i) … as a modal verb.
b) We use *will* when we decide …	ii) … to talk about future facts.
c) *Will* can also be used …	iii) … to talk about an action in progress at a future time.
d) We use *going to* when it is clear …	iv) … something must happen soon.
e) We use *going to* …	v) … for something continuing in the future.
f) We can use the present simple …	vi) … for an action that will be completed by a certain point in the future.
g) We use the future continuous …	vii) … we know or believe will happen.
h) We also use the future continuous …	viii) … to do something at the time of talking.
i) The future perfect is used …	ix) … when explaining future plans.

7 Match each of the following sentences with one of the rules above.
- We're out of milk! Don't worry, I'll get you some.
- The flight leaves at 18.00.
- Dixie will step off the Siberian mainland.
- The dinner will have got cold by the time you sit down.
- It's going to start pouring soon.
- I'm going to leave on time today.
- They'll be swimming in the pool this time next week.
- I'll do that if you want.
- They'll be sleeping for hours yet.

8 Imagine that you are an adventurer and have done some research for a charity in the Arctic. You have been asked to write a report based on your research. Make a sentence about each of the following using one of the future tenses:

a) penguins; reduce numbers
b) thickness; ice
c) Spring; warmer
d) by 2020; ice; less
e) minerals; mined
f) indigenous people; leave
g) polar bears; habitats
h) tourists; more.

Focus on vocabulary

Similes and metaphors

A *simile* is where one thing is compared to another using the words *as* or *like*.

Two examples from the passage:

> It's like an icy wave.
>
> As hard as concrete.

A *metaphor* also compares a word or phrase as if it were something else, e.g.:

> Her skin was ice blue.

Using similes and metaphors helps to make your writing more interesting and descriptive.

9 Say if the following are similes or metaphors.
a) She was as beautiful as a rose.
b) They ran like they were being chased by a tiger.
c) The wind was a raging lion.
d) A wave of terror washed over him.
e) The tears fell like pouring rain.

10 Make a simile and a metaphor out of each of the following.
a) The little girl was as good as _____.
b) The little girl _____.
c) The bag was as heavy as _____.
d) The bag _____.

e) Her eyes were _____.

f) Her eyes _____.

g) The cloud _____.

h) The cloud _____.

i) The water _____.

j) The water _____.

E Let's write

Writing to describe

When you write to describe, you are trying to create a picture for your reader that they would find easy to imagine. The writer in the passage on page 102 describes his experience of travelling in the Arctic and Antarctic.

The words that you use when describing something should be chosen carefully because you don't want your writing to be unnatural. Let's look at some examples from the passage on page 102:

> *... will step off the Siberian mainland and onto the frozen Arctic Ocean ...*

Here the writer is making the idea that the person is stepping from one different place to another and that it is a big step because it is into an Ocean.

> *... Greenland is a paradise for kites ...*

Here the writer is describing how Greenland is not just nice for kite flying but a *paradise* – so making greater emphasis.

We looked at similes and metaphors above and these can also be used in description as they can make your writing come alive.

Look at this piece of writing.

> *The iceberg drifted slowly and heavily through the slow-flowing waters as if it were heavy with child. The winds whipping round it made its progress through the waters slower as it was being pulled in different directions by the pushing of the wind, the pulling of the flow of the waters and the heavy drag of its own weight.*

The writer is trying to get across a picture of an iceberg moving heavily through water.

1 Give four examples of how the writer effectively describes the slow progress of the iceberg.

2 You are now going to write a descriptive essay of about 250 words.

Imagine that you are travelling on a ship through the Arctic and you have been asked by a newspaper to record your travels. Describe part of your trip. Take care with the words that you choose to describe the scenery and the different things that you see.

F Let's do some research

James Hooper and Rob Gauntlett are two men who have finally completed a man-powered journey around the planet. They covered 42 000 km from the North to the South Poles!

You are going to do some further research on their journey and find out the following and more about them:
- who are they – some personal history
- when they started and finished
- what methods of travel they used
- why they travelled
- the route of their journey
- any accidents they might have had
- where they got their financing from
- any other interesting information.

If you find it difficult to find out about these two men, then do your research on some other adventurers who have made their way around the world, either North to South or East to West.

G Let's learn something new

- Gondwana was a super continent more than 200 million years ago. It connected Antarctica to Africa, Australia, India and South America.
- Antarctica has one of the longest mountain ranges in the world, called the Trans-Antarctic Mountains.
- The first person to reach the South Pole was Roald Amundsen in December 1911.

Problem Earth

A Let's start

1 Look at the following bags and say what type each one is. How are they similar or different?

2 Match each sentence with one of the bags above.

What bag am I?

a) Rare animals like snakes and crocodiles are killed in the wild to make me.

b) Little children with little fingers are used to make me, as theirs are the only fingers that can sew on the tiny stones and beads.

c) I am grown in countries like Brazil, Pakistan and Turkey and then chemicals are used to clean me and make me different colours. These chemicals flow into the rivers.

d) Soft, furry animals like baby seals, kangaroos and skunks are killed, often in cruel ways, and only their skin is used.

e) I am made of oil and other chemicals and often used only once and then I am thrown away. It takes years for me to disappear. I can also kill animals as I get caught up in their bodies.

f) I am the best sort because I can be used again and again and I am made of materials that are friendly to the environment.

g) Trees are cut down to make me and often these trees are not replaced, so the soil washes away when it rains, destroying whole areas of land.

h) Animal skin is used to make me; more often than not the animals are specially bred and their meat is used as well.

3 You will find five environmental and other world issues in the word circle on the left. Match each one with the issues in Exercise 2.

4 What other types of world environmental problems can you think of? Think of **four** more and for each one, think how it happens. Use the example to help you.

Global warming	?	?	?	?
The use of cars, and industries, are helping to increase the levels of CO_2 in the atmosphere.				

5 How much do you know about the environment and the problems of our planet? Test yourself!

a) A non-expert person who cares for the environment is:
i) a biologist; ii) an environmentalist; iii) eco-friendly

b) The best way to get to school every day would be:
i) on foot or by bike; ii) by school bus; iii) by car with parents

c) The best fruit you can buy at a supermarket is:
i) exotic imported fruit; ii) local seasonal fruit; iii) healthy fruit

d) The best way to save energy at home in the winter is to:
i) wear a jumper if you are cold; ii) keep the whole house warm;
iii) sit in a hot bath

e) Which cooking method uses the least energy?
i) gas; ii) microwave; iii) electricity

f) Which kind of rain contains chemical waste and causes damage to life?
i) monsoon rain; ii) seasonal rain; iii) acid rain

g) How many trees would 1000 kg of recycled paper save?
i) one tree; ii) 17 trees; iii) 100 trees

h) The best way to wash your clothes is by:
i) hand washing with hot water; ii) machine washing in cold water; iii) machine washing in hot water

i) What term is used to describe where animals can live in safety?
i) conservation; ii) micro home; iii) safe home

j) The term used for the collection of bottles and plastics, etc. to be reused is:
   i) reusing; ii) recycling; iii) reintroducing

k) What doesn't affect the ozone layer?
   i) using spray deodorant; ii) burning coal; iii) sweating

l) Recycling one tin can save enough energy to run a TV for how many hours?
   i) 10 hours; ii) 3 hours; iii) 1 hour

m) The average global temperature since the 1800s has increased by:
   i) 10°C; ii) 0.4 to 0.8°C; iii) 0.8 to 10°C

B Let's read 1

Animals are an important part of our world but, because they cannot protect themselves against their greatest enemy, 'mankind', many species are in danger of extinction all over the world.

1 Look at the following animals and for each one say:
   a) what type of animal it is and why it is in danger
   b) what part of the world it is endangered in.

2 Here are the reasons why and the places where these animals are in danger of extinction. Match them with the animals above. Some can apply to more than one animal. Are they the same as you talked about with your friend?

- Lack of habitat and reduction in vegetation which is natural diet – Australia.

- Meat delicacy – China.

- Overfishing and drift nets – Europe.
- Ivory for medicine and ornaments – Zambia.
- Heads and body parts for collectors – Indonesia.
- Skins and body parts used for ornaments and medicine – worldwide.
- Urbanisation of land means loss of habitat – worldwide.
- Fur for clothes and accessories – Canada.
- Farming for medicine – China.
- Exotic pets – America, Europe, etc.
- Noise pollution causes distress – world's oceans.
- Different species brought in and overtake traditional ones – Northern Europe.

Above, we saw that noise pollution causes distress to marine animals, especially whales. You are going to read a passage about this subject, but first let's see how much you know about the sounds that whales and other marine animals make.

3 Look at the sentences below and say if they are true or false.

a) The voices of whales and other marine animals are different from those of other animals.
b) Marine animals can't see very well in the water.
c) Sound and hearing are important to improve their 'visibility'.
d) They use frequencies that we can't hear.
e) In whales the sound are made through their mouths.
f) Their blowholes are used only for breathing.
g) They use sound to communicate.
h) They can communicate over hundreds of kilometres.
i) They can use sound to 'see'.
j) They can produce an image if they listen to the echo of the sound they sent out.

4 Match the following synonyms from the passage opposite.

a) counter	i) criticises
b) seismic	ii) exactly
c) sonar	iii) cut off/trapped
d) literally	iv) sound navigation
e) strandings	v) amazing
f) navigate	vi) oppose
g) staggering	vii) earthquake
h) condemns	viii) traverse

Noise pollution drowning out world's marine animals

Noise pollution of the world's oceans now poses such a serious threat to marine animals that urgent international action must be taken to counter it, an alarming new International Fund for Animal Welfare (IFAW) report warns today.

The report, 'Ocean Noise: Turn It Down', highlights how steadily-increasing man-made noise – particularly from shipping, sonar and seismic surveys – is interfering with marine mammals' communication, dramatically altering their behaviour and injuring and even killing whales and dolphins.

The report follows growing concern about ocean noise pollution from scientists and international bodies, including the United Nations. It reveals that man-made noise is already making it harder for marine mammals to use their own sounds or echo-location to find food, prey and mates, to navigate and form group bonds.

The report also tells how ocean noise pollution is causing marine mammals to abandon habitats and vital activities such as feeding, as well as altering their surfacing and diving. Some whales have been forced to change their calls as they struggle to make themselves heard, and the distance over which blue whales can communicate has been reduced by a staggering 90%.

IFAW's ocean noise report especially condemns high-intensity sound sources as a major threat, such as seismic surveys and military sonar used by the world's navies to detect submarines. The colossal sounds these emit can injure marine animals and damage their hearing. High-intensity sonar has also been linked by scientists to many fatal strandings of whales and dolphins. The stranding and deaths of 26 dolphins in Cornwall, UK recently followed a Royal Navy exercise nearby, although no specific cause has yet been revealed.

5 Find the following in the passage above and use it to complete a copy of this table.

Three man-made noises:	Four ways the man-made noises are hurting marine animals:	Three groups of people involved in the report:	Three problems that are occuring because mammals can't use their own sound system:
What the man-made noises are made for:	A suggested result of a recent navy exercise:	What the numbers 90 and 26 refer to:	Four ways that mammals are altering their behaviour due to noise:

C # Let's speak and listen

1 How much do you agree or disagree with how animals are used in Section B, Exercise 2 above? With your partner, talk about the following points and decide how much you agree or disagree with the statements. Give reasons for your answers in a table like the one below. Don't worry about the final three columns yet.

	You			Marianna		
	☹	☺	Reasons	☹	☺	Reasons
a) Animals are there for humans to use as they see fit.						
b) If the animal is killed in a humane (not painful) way, what is the problem?						
c) There is no difference between using skin from a cow and using skin from a crocodile.						
d) Killing animals in the wild is no different from killing animals that are farmed.						
e) By nature people will always eat meat.						
f) People will always like to buy products made from animal parts.						
g) Real fur is beautiful so people will always want to buy it.						
h) Not everybody likes cats and dogs as pets, so what is wrong if they have something different and look after it?						
i) It's not wrong to kill exotic animals that can then be used in medicine.						
j) Humans are more important than animals.						
k) If the animals were bred on farms and sold legally then the practice would be acceptable.						
l) People who are caught selling exotic animals should be put in prison.						

2 Now listen to Marianna talking. As you listen, complete the final columns in your table with the information she talks about.

D Let's read 2

1 Do you know what film this is? Do you know what the story is about? Look at the pictures and try to guess the story.

2 Match the sentences and you will find out more about the film.

The film genre is …	… Ape City and imprisoned.
A spaceship with human astronauts …	… Statue of Liberty.
The year is …	… 2006-year voyage.
The astronauts have been on a …	… scientific experiments.
In real life time …	… in a desert.
The astronauts crash landed …	… dirt.
Soon they are chased by …	… the astronauts escape.
They are taken to …	… for Planet of the Apes.
Apes are the master class and …	… civilization through war.
Humans are considered to be …	… Earth all along.
Humans are used for …	… science fiction/thriller.
At the end of the film …	… 3978.
The astronaut discovers a damaged …	… the voyage lasted 18 months.
He realises that he has been on …	… gorillas on horseback.
Humanity had destroyed its own …	… crash lands on a planet.
This paved the way …	… can talk.

3 In the film *Planet of the Apes*, humanity destroyed its own civilization through war. How realistic do you think this ending to the film is? What future do you think there is for humanity with the many problems the world has?

4 Look at the list of events below and with your partner, decide which you think is most likely to happen in the future. Put the sentences in order; starting with what you think is mostly likely to happen first. You may add your own ideas if you think they are more likely.

a) World War III.

b) A nuclear accident will occur.

c) The Earth will be sucked into a black hole.

d) World poverty will end.

e) Pollution in the atmosphere will kill off all oxygen, killing all life forms.

f) Alternative, cleaner and cheap sources of fuel will be found and everybody will have equal access to them.

g) Water will be contaminated and thousands will die.

h) There will be famine due to over-population.

i) People will learn to live together.

j) The Earth will be flooded after global warming melts the polar ice caps.

5 Look at these newspaper stories. Match the stories to the events they are talking about from Exercise 4. There are only three stories but 10 events!

Chemicals from a huge factory in India flowed into the Ganges River this morning killing thousands of people who use it as their main source of drinking water. The government called an emergency session to try to deal with the spiralling problem as thousands of people who live in the area have no other source of drinking water. The government has called on the international community to supply India with bottled drinking water but the immensity of the problem

makes this no small feat. <u>It is expected</u> that the numbers of dead and dying will increase dramatically as the contaminated water seeps into the water system.

News Alert!

<u>It has just been revealed</u> that a nuclear explosion has occurred in France at a nuclear power plant based on the French–German border. As yet <u>the extent of the damage is unknown</u> but the governments of all European countries have issued a stern warning of the dangers as a result of the explosion. The leaders of Europe have told people that as yet they have no clear indication of damage but that people should prepare themselves for the worst and that hiding in cellars and panicking will not help the situation. There has also been a desperate call from all hospitals for all types of blood donors as stocks are very low at the moment.

The United Nations announced today that world poverty is finally a thing of the past. Governments of all countries should celebrate, according to the Secretary General, but at the same time there was the warning that we should not become complacent. <u>It was stated</u> that the main reason for this amazing new world phenomenon was the introduction of genetically-modified crops which over the years <u>have been developed</u> so that they have become resistant to disease and drought. Also, through the coordination and cooperation of the World Crop Plan, selected countries <u>have been chosen</u> to produce a certain quota each year which will cover their own country's needs as well as other countries, that can't produce the necessary amounts.

Focus on grammar

The passive voice

6 Underlined in the news reports above are examples of the passive voice. Match each of the underlined examples with its correct form given below.
   a) Present perfect passive
   b) Present perfect passive
   c) Present perfect passive
   d) Present simple passive
   e) Present simple passive
   f) Past simple passive

7 Say if the following sentences are true about the passive voice.
   a) The passive is formed with the verb *to be* + *past participle*.
   b) *Am*, *is* and *are* are forms of the verb *to be*.
   c) Both regular and irregular verbs have past participles.
   d) The past participle of regular verbs ends with -ed.
   e) The past participle is another way of saying the past tense.
   f) The past participle of *throw* is *threw*.
   g) The passive focuses more on the action of a sentence.
   h) It is not always necessary to know who the agent (the person who does the action) is.
   i) The passive is used often in formal and technical English.
   j) The passive is used when the person is more important than the action.

8 Change the following sentences into the passive.
   a) People expect him to be the next President.
      He _____
   b) Firemen have reported that the fire is out of control.
      It _____
   c) Many people believe that saving money is better than spending.
      It _____
   d) The local government knocked the cemetery down without consulting anyone first.
      The _____
   e) Christians throughout the world celebrate Easter every year.
      Easter _____
   f) NASA has sent up another satellite for the weather.
      Another _____
   g) People who loved the book directed the film *Lord of the Rings*.
      The _____
   h) Corrupt governments waste a lot of their country's resources.
      A _____
   i) People would buy electric cars if they were easily available.
      Electric _____
   j) OPEC would reduce the price of oil if there were less demand.
      The _____

Focus on vocabulary

Countries and nationalities

In the newspaper stories on pages 114–115, we saw the following:

India / French / German / Europe

9 Which is a country? Which is a group of countries? Which is a nationality?

10 Now, what are the following?

| Mongolian | Japan | Afghanistan | Turk |
| Sudanese | Korea | Irish | Dutch |

11 Find either the country or the nationality for the following.

Country	Nationality
	Afghan
	Azerbaijani
Belarus	
	Belgian
Congo	
Cyprus	
Denmark	
	Djiboutian
	Equadorean
Egypt	
France	

Country	Nationality
Holland	
Iceland	
	Irish
	Kazakh
Laos	
Liechtenstein	
Nepal	
	Omani
	Polish
Scotland	
Switzerland	

E Let's write

Newspaper writing

The purpose of a newspaper is to report news of all kinds to all types of readers. The reader could be any age, gender, educational background, etc.

Different newspapers are written with a different audience in mind.

1 Look at the questions that have been answered below about the first newspaper story in Exercise 5.

2 Now your teacher will give you three other newspapers. Complete a copy of the table in the same way for each newspaper.

	Example from Exercise 5
Describe the layout, e.g. colours used, pictures, etc.	Columns. Pictures used in main stories.
Who would you say were the main readers? Why?	Adults and serious readers. Use of the passive.
Does the newspaper support any political party?	Not obvious.
Describe how it is different from the other newspapers.	n/a
Describe how it is the same as the other newspapers.	n/a
What kinds of stories are included mostly in the newspaper?	Current stories.
Look at the language used by the newspaper. • Is it formal/informal? • Simple/difficult language? • Factual/opinion?	Formal. Difficult. Factual.

3 Think of a recent national or international event. It could be political, social, sporting, etc. You are going to write a newspaper article about it.

Write about 250 words. Find out some details of the story before you begin. Present your piece in newspaper style.

F Let's do some research

What do **you** think is the most serious world problem?

You are going to do some research into it and prepare a presentation.

You can do it by yourself or with your friend.

Before you begin make sure:
- you have plenty of facts about the subject
- you have collected any pictures that you might use to support your project
- you know how you are going to present your ideas
- you know who your audience is going to be
- you know what approach you're going to take in your project, e.g. formal/informal, informative, etc.
- you think about the methods you are going to use to attract your readers attention, e.g. use of colours, headlines, catchy phrases, etc.

Prepare your presentation and then go over your ideas with your teacher before you begin.

G Let's learn something new

- Starlings, sparrows and pigeons are the most common city birds and are the most adaptable to their environment.
- Acid rain has been dealt with for over a decade with some success.
- Globally there are more than one billion overweight adults; at least 300 million of them are obese.

Dance and movement

A Let's start

1 Look at the dancers and talk about them with your partner.

- Which type of dancing shown in the pictures do you like and which do you not like? Why?
- How are the styles of dancing the same as or different from each other?
- Have you seen any types of dancing like this?
- Would you like to go and see dancing like this? Why/why not?

2 What is 'dance' to you? Talk about it with your partner.

3 Look at the following quotations about dance. Decide if you agree with them or not. Are the quotations the same as or different from your own feelings about dance?

'A child sings before it speaks, dances almost before it walks. Music is in our hearts from the beginning.'
Pamela Brown

'The dance is a poem of which every movement is a word.'
Mata Hari

'Dance is your pulse, your heartbeat, your breathing. It's like the rhythm of your life. It's the expression in time and movement.'
Jacques D' Ambroise

4 Think of all the different reasons why people dance. Make a list.

5 Here are four pictures. Each one shows a different reason why people dance. Are they the same as the ideas you talked about with your partner?

6 Here are eight reasons why people dance, but to find out what they are, you have to work out what the code is!

α	β	γ	δ	ε	ζ	η	θ	ι	κ	λ	μ	ν
a	b	c	d	e	f	g	h	i	j	k	l	m
ξ	o	π	ρ	ς	σ	τ	u	φ	χ	ψ	ω	-
n	o	p	q	r	s	t	u	v	w	x	y	z

a) ξατιοξαμ δαξγεσ

b) εξτεσταιξνεξτ

c) χεδδιξησ

d) σεμζ - πμεασυςε

e) πθωσιγαμ εψεσγιςε

f) γονπετιτιοξσ

g) γυμτυςαμ

h) νεξταμ εψεσγιςε

7 Can you think of any other reason why people dance? Draw a spider diagram with 'Types of dancing' in the centre. How many different types of dancing can you think of, e.g. ballet?

countryandwestern
jazztapswingmodernlatinfolkflamencohip-hopballet

8 There are ten types of dancing in the word circle on the left. Find them and then match each one to one of the descriptions below.

   a) This expressive dance mixes percussive footwork with intricate hand, arm and body movement and is a Spanish art.

   b) This dance comes from South America and has movements that are made with the intention of attracting the opposite sex.

   c) This dance serves as a backbone for many other styles of dancing.

   d) Dancers wear special shoes fitted with metal pieces.

   e) A variety of dances that have been developed by groups or communities.

   f) Lively dance style in which couples dance and move energetically together.

   g) Developed from a cultural movement in the US from mainly African Americans and Latinos.

   h) Dancing with mostly cowboys and mostly American influence.

   i) Rejects many of the strict rules of classical ballet and focuses on expressing the inner self.

   j) Fun dance style that uses bold, dramatic body movements.

9 With your partner, talk about the following statements. How much do you agree or disagree with them?

   ● Dance in our society is mainly for girls.
   ● If a boy goes to ballet school, his friends will laugh at him.
   ● All dancers are athletes.
   ● A male dancer is much fitter and stronger than the average man.
   ● Dancing is much more accepted in some cultures than in others.
   ● Everybody can and should dance.
   ● Dance is another form of expression like music or painting.

10 Have you seen the film *Billy Elliot*? Do you know what the story is about?

Look at the words which are connected with the story and see if you can work out what happens in the film.

ballet – boxing – miner – English mining town – no money – mother dead

11 Match the sentence halves and you will have an outline of the story. Check how much of the story you got right in Exercise 10.

Billy Elliot is an …	… had an artistic streak which was passed down to Billy.
He lives in an imaginary town …	… accepts that his son is passionate about dancing.
Billy's father is a …	… moves to live in London.
His mother who died years ago …	… to become a champion boxer.
Billy's father wants him …	… 11-year-old boy.
But Billy has seen and wants …	… Matthew Bourne's *Swan Lake*.
So Billy secretly starts taking …	… can't accept the idea of Billy as a dancer.
Billy's brother and father …	… to do ballet.
After seeing Billy dance, his father …	… striking coal miner with no money.
He takes Billy to London and the …	… ballet lessons with the money given to him for boxing lessons.
Billy is accepted at the school and …	… Royal Ballet School where he has an audition.
The film ends 14 years later when …	… in the industrial area of Britain.
He dances the lead role in …	… his father sees him dance professionally.

B Let's read 1

1 Look at the following robots and match them to their names.

HRP-2 *or* Promet   R2D2   Dalek

1

2

3

2 With your partner, talk about what a robot can and can't do and write your ideas down.

Did you include dancing?

3 We are going to look at a story where a robot has been taught to dance!

What is the name of that robot? You have its name in Exercise 1. Find it in the text.

Japanese teach robot to dance

Scientists in Japan have taught a human-sized robot to imitate the steps of a dancer. They say the prancing dancebot could be used to record the movements of traditional dances that are being lost as their performers die off.

To demonstrate the robot's prowess, the team programmed the 1.5 metre tall machine to imitate the graceful sways and whirls of the Aizu Bandaisan, a Japanese folk routine. To prove its accuracy, the robot can perform alongside a human dancer. And despite its "Terminator" appearance, the robot is remarkably lifelike.

Two colleagues at Tokyo University taught the dancebot – named HRP-2 or Promet – by using video-capture techniques to record human dance movements. They managed to directly copy human movement, which is very difficult because the joints of the robot are very different from the joints of a human. Nonetheless, its rendition of the mainly upper-body dance is impressive, although it has difficulty with complicated leg movements. Despite this, if it can be tweaked to handle more leggy folk dances, it may be popular with purists who want to see traditional dances preserved.

When asked for their opinion about the robot, a human said, "It's like language. If you think about the development of language, we are constantly developing new slang and dropping old slang," whereas another said, "My impression is that there would still be a human element lacking. The robot would still look, for the want of a better word, robotic."

The fascination between dancers and robots is not new, as shown in the ballet 'Coppélia', which was first performed in 1870 and is about a man who falls in love with a life-sized doll. It might be tempting to some to imagine a whole corps de ballet of robots performing 'Swan Lake', but it's unlikely machines will replace human performers altogether, since the focus of the theatre arts is the relationship between the audience and the imperfect human performer.

4 Here are the answers based on the passage opposite – but what are the questions?

   a) In 1870.
   b) The first but not the second human.
   c) Two scientists in Japan.
   d) It can imitate the movements of a Japanese folk dance.
   e) Terminator.
   f) By using video capture techniques.
   g) The joints.
   h) Yes, but not the lower part.
   i) No, they think people prefer human performers.
   j) To preserve dances.

C Let's speak and listen

1 Classical ballet is often based on very old and very traditional stories. Here are four very popular and famous ballets. With your partner, talk about the stories and see how much you know about them. Copy and complete the table with as much information as you can.

	Giselle	Coppélia	Swan Lake	The Nutcracker
Music written by:	Adolphe Adams	Delibes		
Main setting:			Prince's castle and forest	
Storyline:				Christmas fantasy with animals
Main characters:		Coppélia and Franz		
Some features of the ballet:	Ghostly dancers			National dances
Story's ending:				Clara wakes from the dream
First performed in:		1870	1877	
Story based on:	French poem		Russian folk tale	

2 Now listen for the full details of the ballets and check your answers. Complete the table with information that you didn't know.

D | Let's read 2

It is not possible to say when dance became part of human culture but it has always been an important part of ceremonies, celebrations and entertainment from the earliest times. Archaeologists have found evidence of dance as far back as 9000 years ago in India and in Egypt from about 3300 BC. But ethnic dances vary from one part of the world to another.

With your partner you are going to think and talk about different ethnic dances and the different characteristics of each one, but before you do that …

1 How much do you know about the ethnic dances of your country? Copy and complete the table.

Questions	Answers
What is your country's name?	
What are the names of at least two ethnic dances from your country?	
What are most of your country's ethnic dances based on?	
What sort of costumes are worn by the dancers?	
What sort of music is played?	
Who does most of the dancing?	
How famous internationally is your country's ethnic dancing?	
What are the origins of your country's ethnic dances?	
What features are characteristic of your country's ethnic dances?	

2 Now look at the pictures of the following ethnic dancers and match them with the region in the world they come from.

Write down anything you know about each country's ethnic dance.

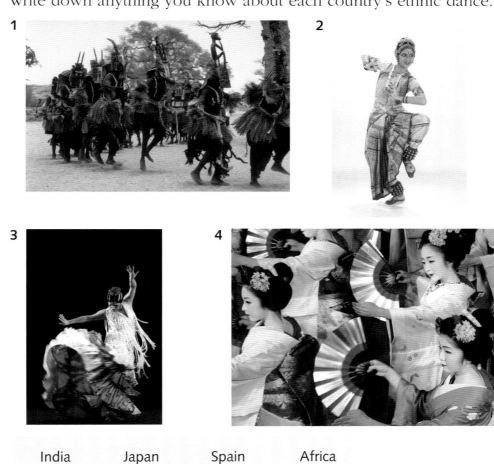

India   Japan   Spain   Africa

3 Now read the following and add more information to your notes.

India

In India, which has a long history of music and dance, dances celebrate various festivals and rites of passage. The most important is a Hindu classical dance-drama where one woman uses a great variety of bodily movements, which are accompanied by rhythms stamped out with the feet.

Japan

Traditional dances have been performed for centuries in Japan. No and Kabuki, which are among the best-known dance forms, both combine mime and dance steps, and are dance-dramas. Unlike dancing in the western world, which can be very fast, Japanese dancing is very formal and moves at a slow and stately pace.

Spain

Some native dances from Spain can be traced back to Greek times. Spanish dancers were known throughout the Roman Empire for their artistry. Perhaps the best-known Spanish dance is the flamenco, which is a gypsy dance thought to be of Indian or Persian origin.

Africa

The origins of African dance are lost in antiquity, but it is known that tribal people throughout Africa relied on dance to a remarkable degree. Dances, which were an integral part of everyday life, were used to express joy and grief, to invoke prosperity and avoid disaster, as part of religious rituals, and purely as pastimes.

Focus on grammar

Relative clauses and pronouns

A relative clause gives a sentence extra information. It uses specific words and phrases depending on what the extra information contains, e.g.

The girl, who just walked into the room, is my older sister.

Sometimes, a relative adverb is used to replace a pronoun + preposition:

- when = in/on which
- where = in/at which
- why = for which

4 Complete the pronoun/adverb column below with words from the box.

who / which / that / when / whose / where / why

Pronoun/adverb	Use
	Used for people.
	For things and animals.
	Refers to expressions of time.
	Refers to expressions of place.
	Refers to a reason.
	Refers to possession.
	Used for people, animals or things.

5 Complete the sentences using an appropriate word.
  a) Those are the children _____ parents didn't come to the meeting.
  b) The place _____ I met him has now closed down.
  c) Those are the cars _____ were involved in the accident last night.
  d) The reason _____ we met him doesn't exist now.
  e) The person _____ stole Maria's purse is to come forward, please.
  f) The newspaper, _____ we want it, is never there.
  g) Can you see my cat _____ is lying in the sunshine?

6 Find four examples of relative clauses in the passage on pages 127–128.

Defining relative clauses give more information that is essential to the meaning of the main sentence. The clause is not between commas, e.g.

> People who dance need to be healthy.

Who, which and *that* can be omitted when they are the object of the relative clause, e.g.

> This is the remains of the book (which) the dog ate.

Non-defining relative clauses give more information and are not essential to the meaning of the main sentence. The relative pronouns and adverbs cannot be omitted in this form, e.g.

> Ballet dancers, who dance regularly, need to be healthy to perform effectively.

7 Join the sentences using the appropriate relative pronoun/adverb and using commas where necessary, e.g.

> Nureyev / famous ballet dancer / defected from the USSR.

> *Nureyev, who was a famous ballet dancer, defected from the USSR.*

  a) Children / study ballet / must start very young.
  b) The New York City Ballet / founded in 1948 / still exists today.
  c) The woman / purse you found on the floor / lives in the flat downstairs.

d) The Coliseum in London / a famous ballet hall / was recently renovated.

e) *Billy Elliot* / film made in 2000 / is now also a stage musical.

f) The summer / I went to Egypt / I got sunburnt.

Focus on vocabulary

Parts of the body

8 How many body parts can you think of? You have one minute to write as many as possible, e.g. nose, mouth.

9 Match these body words with their definition below.

snore	blush	sneeze	chew
perspire	wink	sigh	suck
tremble	swallow	yawn	blink
frown	rumble	cough	

a) You do this after you put some food in your mouth.

b) You do this when you have a tickle in your throat.

c) You do this when you have a hard sweet in your mouth.

d) You do this after you have been dancing on a hot day.

e) You do this when you are not happy with something.

f) You do this when you are relieved about something.

g) You do this when you have something in your eye.

h) Your stomach does this when you are hungry.

i) You do this when you are embarrassed about something.

j) You do this sometimes when you are fast asleep.

k) You do this with food in your mouth that is too big too swallow.

l) You do this when you are frightened.

m) You do this when you are tired.

n) You do this when something goes up your nose.

o) You do this with one eye as a message to someone else.

E Let's write

Organising your writing

When writing a text which is not a play, poem, story, etc. but is a report, an article which gives information or a newspaper article, etc., we need to plan our writing in a different way.

If we look at the passage on pages 127–128 about ethnic dances we can see that:

a) the passage has been divided by headings
b) the paragraph under each heading will only deal with that particular topic
c) the reader will know exactly what they will read about.

Other ways to organise your writing are:

i) Use paragraphs when you want to write about a new idea.
ii) Use topic sentences at the beginning of each paragraph. A topic sentence usually comes at the beginning of the paragraph and introduces what the paragraph will be about.
iii) The beginning of your work should catch your reader's interest and let them know what they are going to read about.
iv) Use vocabulary that helps you organise your text, e.g. first, to begin with, however, nonetheless, despite that, finally, in conclusion, etc.
v) Know how you are going to end your writing and what ideas you are going to put in the final conclusion.

The writing task you are going to do now will be part of your 'Let's do some research' section.

You are going to research a given topic and present it in the style given above, including some or all of the features.

F Let's do some research

You are going to research a particular dance style that interests you. This dance style could be anything from classical ballet to hip-hop dancing.

You will organise your text so that it includes all or most of the features as given in the 'Let's write' section.

Your writing will be organised under some of the following headings:
- Introduction
- Origins and history (of the dance style chosen)
- Features and characteristics (of the dance style)
- Current performances
- Main audience and performers
- Conclusion.

G Let's learn something new

- The first ballerina to dance on her toes (*pointe*) was Cecilia Castellini in 1778.
- Belly dancing dates back as far as the 14th century.
- The word 'dance' comes from the Sanskrit 'tanha' and means 'joy of life'.

Unit 11 Cinema

Let's start

1 Look at the following pictures and talk about them with your partner.

What do the pictures show?

What is happening in each of the pictures?

What do you know about the development of cinema?

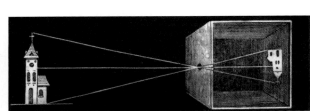

2 Match the information given opposite, about how cinema developed, to the dates in the table.

470–390 BC	965–1039 BC	1878	1895	1920s	1950s	1970s	2000s

a) English photographer Eadweard Muybridge photographs a horse in fast motion.

b) First films are silent with subtitles and music played separately by a pianist.

c) Blockbusters/special effects/film advertising/recognisable cast (actors) all become important.

d) The Chinese philosopher Mozi first mentions and discovers the principle of a simple camera.

e) Lumière brothers in Paris publicly show the world's first motion picture.

f) Use of computers for special effects. Spectacular battle scenes. Computer graphics used for special effects.

g) Moving cinema is recognised as being a large-scale entertainment industry.

h) Arab scientist Abu Ali Al-Hasan builds the first pinhole camera.

3 How well do you know your films? Choose the correct answer.
   a) Kung Fu Panda wore:
   i) trousers; **ii)** shorts; **iii)** a T-shirt
   b) In the film *Madagascar* there were _____ penguins.
   i) three; **ii)** two; **i)** one
   c) Walt Disney died in:
   i) 1946; **ii)** 1960; **ii)** 2006
   d) The characters Mewtwo, Raichu, Pikachu and Cubone are from:
   i) *Toy Story*; **ii)** *Ninja Turtles*; **iii)** *Pokemon*
   e) *Ratatouille* was a film about:
   i) France; **ii)** vegetables; **iii)** a rat
   f) The last animated Disney feature to be painted entirely by hand was:
   i) *The Little Mermaid* (1989); **ii)** *Sleeping Beauty* (1959);
   iii) *Aladdin* (1992)
   g) Shrek's wife used to be a:
   i) queen; **ii)** working girl; **iii)** princess
   h) The cat in *Garfield* was:
   i) white; **ii)** black; **iii)** ginger
   i) Lucy in *The Chronicles of Narnia* walked through:
   i) a wardrobe; **ii)** an underground station; **iii)** a tree
   j) Snow White bit into a _____ apple:
   i) green; **ii)** red; **iii)** yellow
   k) In *Lord of the Rings*, Frodo Baggins is played by:
   i) Michael Marver; **ii)** Wood Elijah; **iii)** Elijah Wood
   l) Which trilogy ended up at World's End?
   i) *Pirates of the Caribbean*; **ii)** *Lord of the Rings*; **iii)** *Shrek*

m) What film company has a mountain as its logo:
i) Universal; ii) MGM; iii) Paramount

n) In the film *Bugs*, they were attacked by:
i) humans; ii) grasshoppers; iii) wasps

4 Look at some of the terminology used in films – how much do you know?

Match the word with its meaning.

Terminology	Definition
Scriptwriter	When the reel in the camera starts to go round.
Director	Does the faces and hair of the actors/actresses.
To roll	Oversees the entire process of making the film.
Action	Positioning the camera near the face of the actor.
Take	Actors told to start performing.
Cut	Camera at a long distance from the subject.
Close up	When a scene is being filmed at the moment.
Long shot	Writes the dialogue of the film.
Art director	Is responsible for the film's scenery and sets.
Make-up artist	When the director orders filming of a scene to be stopped.

B Let's read 1

1 Copy the table opposite and decide which pieces of the following information go into the correct boxes.

Adventure/comedy	Fight against evil	Daniel Radcliffe
Fantasy/adventure	$472 000 000	$428 000 000
Superhero fights evil	Brad Pitt	Tobey Maguire
Tom Cruise	Peter Jackson	Fantasy literature
$1 002 310 263	Johnny Depp	Magical chocolate factory
Pirates' adventures	Earth invaded by aliens	About a magical ring
Superhero fights evil	$892 000 000	Johnny Depp
$890 900 000	Christian Bale	Children's fantasy
Science fiction	Married couple hired to kill each other	$20 m
$591 000 000	Fiction/fantasy	$1 119 100 000
Fantasy literature	Action/comedy	$38 m
$1 066 200 000		$15 m

Rank	Name of film	Genre	Main actors/director	Story	Total gross	Single salary
1	Lord of the Rings – The Return of the King					
2	Pirates of the Caribbean – Dead Man's Chest					
3	The Dark Knight					
4	Spiderman 3					
5	War of the Worlds					$100m
6	Charlie and the Chocolate Factory					$18m
7	Mr & Mrs Smith					
8	Harry Potter and the Goblet of Fire					$11m

2 Look at the salaries given to the actors and directors for the films above and compare them with the following annual salaries.

Specialist doctor: $166 211

Specialist nurse: $63 655

Head teacher: $176 820

Dustman: $17 000

3 Now talk about the following with your partner.
  a) How do you feel about the salaries that are paid out to actors/directors? Why do you feel this way?
  b) Do you think that they should be paid such high salaries? Why/why not?
  c) Do you think a film is only successful because of who the main actor is? Why/why not?
  d) Why do you think film companies pay out such large salaries?
  e) Do you think a top actor is worth this salary? Why/why not?
  f) How do you think a specialist doctor or nurse would feel if they were to compare their salaries with those of actors/directors?
  g) Think about what training and work a specialist doctor/nurse, head teacher, etc. does for their salary, compared with an actor.

4 You are now going to read a passage about actors' salaries. Read it and check your answers from Exercise 1 in the column 'Single salary'.

Hollywood stars meet the real world. It's pay cuts all round

Hollywood stars are being forced to take pay cuts as the major studios are pulling the plug on big-budget projects.

With box office takings down 5.2 per cent and the cost of making movies ballooning because of added expenses for digital enhancement and global marketing, studios are refusing to meet stars' financial demands. In addition, several high-profile films due to go into production have suddenly disappeared from view.

Studios have taken note of the fact that only three of the 10 highest-grossing films recently – 'War of the Worlds', 'Charlie and the Chocolate Factory' and 'Mr and Mrs Smith' – were star-driven. The rest of the major hits – such as 'Star Wars Episode III – Revenge of the Sith', 'Harry Potter and the Goblet of Fire' and 'The Chronicles of Narnia' – had no stellar names, or fat salaries to speak of. In addition, many recent Oscar nominees for best actors worked for rock-bottom wages. The last of the big paydays went to 'Lord of the Rings' director Peter Jackson, who was paid a reported $20m plus 20 per cent of the gross for 'King Kong' made by Universal.

Now studios are making sure that before any stars or directors take money from the film, they get their cut. Sony refused to give the green light for the romantic comedy 'The Holiday' until Cameron Diaz agreed to a "cash break-even" deal. Even Tom Cruise, who normally collects around 25 per cent of his films' gross profits agreed to take a much lower cut for 'Mission Impossible 3' when Paramount was faced with a massively bloated budget and at one stage threatened to cancel the project. And Brad Pitt is another one who has taken a big cut in pay, from his customary fee of up to $30m down to just $1 326 154.42 for his latest.

Former 20th Century Fox chairman Bill Mechanic describes it as a long overdue rationalisation of the business. "In the past you paid someone a lot of money to star in a movie and then you spent a lot of money to make a movie and then you lost money."

Another studio executive said, "Movies no longer need big star names to make money. With most studios having to answer to larger parent companies, their main aim now is to assess financial risk and that means making movies that cost less."

5 Match the following words on the left to the words/phrases on the
right, which are taken from the passage.

stellar	the go ahead
rationalisation	total sum
assess financial risk	normal
pulling the plug	swollen
big budget projects	good reason
ballooning	putting an end to something
gross	famous
green light	work out the dangers
bloated	expensive plans
customary	getting larger

6 Make complete sentences by matching the phrases. You will then
have a summary of the passage.

a) Only some of the most
recent successful films …

b) Most of the top films …

c) Reducing salaries is …

d) Hollywood now …

e) Peter Jackson was one …

f) Films didn't use to …

g) Films don't need big actors …

h) Movies need to cost less …

i) Paramount …

j) Movies are much more …

i) … because of greater costs.

ii) … to make big money.

iii) … don't pay huge salaries
any more.

iv) … nearly had to cancel its
plans.

v) … plans to pay less to
actors.

vi) … had famous actors.

vii) … expensive to make than
in the past.

viii) … make a profit.

ix) … something that should
have happened long ago.

x) … of the last to get a high
salary.

7 a) Write five questions based on the passage opposite.
  b) Give your questions to your partner to answer.
  c) Your partner will give you their five questions.
  d) Write the answers to your partner's questions.
  e) Check both sets of answers together.

Let's speak and listen

1 With your partner, discuss the following questions and complete a copy of the table with your partner's answers.

Questions	Your partner's answers	Sara's answers	Paolo's answers
What is the best film you've ever seen? Why was it the best?			
What is the worst film you've ever seen? Why was it the worst?			
Who is your favourite actor? Name two films they have been in.			
What genre of film do you generally like?			Fantasy
Do you prefer children's films or films for adults?			Children's
Who do you enjoy going to the cinema with?		My friends	
If you were to be the main character in a film, who would it be?		Lady Eowyn from *Lord of the Rings*	
Who do you think is one of the kindest characters in film? Why do you think they are kind?			
Who do you think is one of the cruellest characters in film? Why do you think they are the cruellest?			
If you were to make a film, what would it be about?		The book *Noughts and Crosses*, which is about black and white people	
Do you think films influence how people act? Why/why not?			
Who do you think makes the best films? Why?			
Do you prefer watching films on TV or at the cinema? Why?			
Would you like to be part of the film industry? Yes/No. If yes, in what capacity?			I would rather act than actually organise a film.

2 Now listen to Sara and Paolo answer the same questions. Complete your table with their answers.

D Let's read 2

1 What do the following pictures have in common? What are their names?

1   2   3   4

2 Match the child to the adult in the pictures.

3 Think of four other children who appear in modern-day films.

4 With your partner, talk about the following:
● How do you feel about children becoming actors?
● Would you like to be a child actor? Why/why not?
● Do you know anybody who is a child actor?
● What sort of lives do you think child actors have?
● Do you think that most child actors become actors in their adult lives?
● What sort of pressures do you think child actors have?

5 Look at the names of the following actors. Do you know who they are?

Do you know anything about them? Copy the table below and match the information with the correct name. One of the sentences can apply to both columns.

The Olsens	Macaulay Culkin

● Starred in films like *Home Alone* and *Uncle Buck*.
● They are twins.

- Became famous after 'Mary-Kate and Ashley' films.
- Separated from parents and got married at 18.
- Own huge business selling fashion and beauty products.
- Suffering from illness anorexia nervosa.
- One of the highest-paid child actors of all time.
- Became addicted to drugs.

6 Look at these facts about children in films and advertisements. Talk about them with your partner.
- A child can earn over $50 000 just to appear in a national commercial.
- A child (whatever the age) needs to behave professionally when auditioning (applying for the place).
- Approximately one third of all adverts have children appearing in them.
- Demanding parents often push their child into the acting scene.
- No payment is made unless the child is booked to play a role.
- A child usually needs to have some training and experience before they audition.

7 We have seen that the road to fame for children as actors can be both good and bad. You are going to read an article about some child actors.

Find one actor from the pictures on page 139 who is mentioned in the passage.

What good and bad things are mentioned about child actors?

Child actors

The life of a child actor seems very glamorous – travelling the world and working with famous actors – but it is also very hard work.

Shirley Temple was one of the first and most famous child actors. Born in 1928, by 1950 she had starred in almost 60 films, some written especially for her. She was spotted at the age of three at a dance class by a film director and made her first film in the same year. Her blonde ringlets and dimples were her trademarks, as well as her talent for tap dancing.

Temple's success pulled struggling film company 20th Century Fox away from the brink of bankruptcy. The film company attempted to broaden her appeal by altering her birth certificate to state she was a year younger than her actual age. This made her talents all the more impressive.

Shirley Temple went on to have a successful career in politics and diplomacy. She held the position of US Chief of Protocol, and was ambassador to Ghana and subsequently Czechoslovakia.

Jackie Coogan, born in 1914, was the first child actor to work in Hollywood. He was spotted by Charlie Chaplin and had his first acting role in 1917. He later starred as 'Kid' alongside Charlie Chaplin in 'The Kid' (made in 1921). Coogan earned millions of dollars in the 1920s, which was supposed to be put aside in a trust fund for the actor. In the 1930s Coogan lost popularity and film offers began to dry up. Coogan's mother and stepfather had squandered the child's earnings, leading to a court battle and eventually the introduction of 'Coogan's Law' in 1939, which was designed to protect child actors' earnings by placing the money in a court-administered trust fund until they reach maturity.

Child actors face many other problems. Many are unable to cope psychologically with the rejection they face by film companies once they reach puberty. Others find themselves depressed by pushy, over-ambitious parents and alienated from their peers.

Focus on grammar

Comparisons

8 Find four pieces of information in the passage that compare the two actors Shirley Temple and Jackie Coogan. Use a table like the one below to organise your thoughts.

Shirley Temple	Jackie Coogan
Born in 1928	Born in 1914

9 Find an example in the passage of:
   a) the comparative form
   b) the superlative form.

10 Answer true or false about the following sentences.
   a) The comparative form is only made by adding *-er* to the adverb or adjective.
   b) The superlative is formed by adding *-est* and *the most* to the adjective or adverb.
   c) Adjectives and adverbs with two or more syllables normally take *more/most*.
   d) The superlative form compares more than two things.

e) We use *than* after a comparative form.

f) We usually use *the* before a superlative form.

g) The irregular adjective *good* changes to *better* and *best* in the comparative and superlative forms.

h) We would use the form *as ... as* to talk about two things that are the same.

i) The form *as ... as* cannot be used in the negative.

j) Similes and metaphors are also used to compare things.

11 Now write four sentences using the comparative and superlative forms about the two actors from Exercise 5, e.g.

Macaulay Culkin was born earlier than the Olsens.

12 Look at the following and make either comparative or superlative sentences.

a) Cinema – TV

b) Mickey Rooney – Judy Garland – Shirley Temple

c) Child actors – adult actors

d) The Olsen twins – Macaulay Culkin

e) Fantasy – science fiction – adventure

f) Silent films – blockbusters – digital enhancement.

Focus on vocabulary

Guessing meaning

Remember that the following may help you to guess the meaning of a word if you don't understand it.

● The immediate context – look at the other words around the unfamiliar word to help you understand it.

● Grammatical clues – is it a noun, a verb, etc.? This may help you understand the meaning of the unknown word.

● Similarity to other words that you know in English.

● The use of a prefix or a suffix may help you.

● Similarity to a word in a different language.

Failing all that, and if the word is a key word in the sentence and prevents you from understanding the whole meaning of the sentence, use a dictionary!

13 Here are 18 words and phrases from the passage. Match them with their meanings.

Words/expressions	Meanings
glamorous	a negative response
ringlets	brand name
dimples	wasted
trademark	adulthood
the brink of bankruptcy	friends
broaden	changing
altering	little curls
diplomacy	peace-keeping
protocol	on the edge of economic failure
subsequently	controlled by law
trust fund	accepted way of behaviour
squandered	elegant
psychologically	attractive marks on cheeks
peers	increase/widen
alienated	afterwards
rejection	savings account
court administered	mentally
maturity	separated

E Let's write

Writing a film review

When you write a film review it should be a mixture of fact and opinion.

1 Read this film review and then say if the categories that follow are fact or opinion.

The Chronicles of Narnia: Prince Caspian (PG)

A year after their first exciting adventure in Narnia, Peter, Susan, Edmund and Lucy are pulled back by Susan's magic horn. They find that hundreds of years have passed, and Narnia is now ruled by the bloodthirsty General Miraz, uncle to the true heir, Prince Caspian, now in exile. Now the children must find Caspian and help him depose Miraz.

Aslan, grown in stature, appears later in the story to Lucy who is the most magical of the four siblings.

The real fans of Narnia will be back to see the film a second and third time, while others will also love it.

Starring: Ben Barnes, Georgie Henley, Skandar Keynes, William Moseley, Anna Popplewell.

Adventure Fantasy   Time: 144 minutes   Our rating: *****

Category	Fact?	Opinion?
The title		
The certificate	PG	
Film genre		
The actors		
The story		
Length of film		
The best bits		
Favourite character		
Rating		

2 Now think of your favourite film and write a review about it in approximately 130 words. Use the format and hints above to help you.

F Let's do some research

Charlie Chaplin was one of the earliest and most popular actors. He appeared in many films at the beginning of the 20th century. You are going to do some research on him based on these categories:

- His full name
- Where he was born
- When he was born
- His achievements other than acting
- Length of his career
- Main known character
- How main character was portrayed
- Best films
- Awards won
- Family life
- Legacy
- See if you can find a picture of him to add to your research.

G Let's learn something new

- *Lost* is the most expensive television show ever filmed.
- The first Oscar for Special Effects was awarded in 1940.
- Hollywood used to be called Hollywoodland.

Unit 12 Every picture tells a story

A Let's start

1 Look carefully at the following photographs and put them in chronological order. Start with the oldest first and the most modern last.

1900s   1960s   1980s   2000s

1

2

3

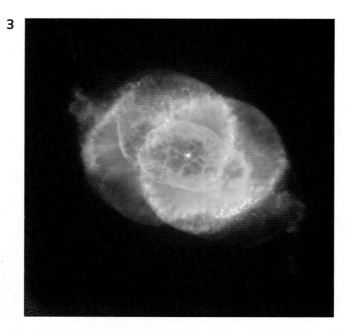

4

2 Answer the questions based on the photographs.
  a) How are the photos different from each other?
  b) What helped you decide the chronological order of the photos?
  c) How might the photos have been taken in each situation?
  d) How has the equipment changed from the first photo to the last?
  e) How might the type of person who took the first photos have
     changed by the later photos?

A photograph can be two different things:

● an image – something that you just see
● a story or information about a person, era, etc.

3 Look at the photograph below and look at the details in it. It can either be just a picture of 11 men or it could be more. Say if you agree with the statements below and give reasons for your ideas.

- They are in America.
- They are builders.
- They are building a skyscraper.
- They are immigrants (moved to live in America from other countries).
- The photo was taken in the 1930s.
- The men are having a break.
- They have a very dangerous job.
- The men do not seem worried about the danger of their job.

B Let's read 1

1 We have seen that photographs can be a very powerful and effective tool, but this has not always been the case.

With your partner, talk about how the role of photography in our lives has changed. Use the questions below to talk about the subject and complete your own copy of the table.

Question	Then	Now
Describe the equipment used to take photographs.		
Describe the people who take most of the photographs.		
Describe the process of how photographs are developed.		

Question	Then	Now
Describe the occasions when photographs are taken.		
Talk about the cost of photographs.		
Talk about the content of photographs, e.g. people, scenery, etc.		
Talk about how photographs are composed, e.g. how natural/ unnatural, etc.		
Talk about the value of photographs.		

One area where photography has become a very effective and powerful tool is in the world of the media because it can bring images to millions of people – this would never have been possible before. An example of this is powerful images of human suffering around the world. The idea is that the visual image will affect people more than any written report or event.

You are going to read an article about a photographer called James Nachtwey, who used his photographs with the intention of raising awareness about the disease tuberculosis (TB).

2 How much do you know about TB? Say if the following are true or false. Then find the correct answers in the passage.
  a) You can die from TB.
  b) TB kills more people than malaria.
  c) It is quite easy to treat TB.
  d) A lot of people in the West know about TB.
  e) Extra funding is needed to control TB.
  f) TB is one of the oldest-known diseases.
  g) TB has killed about two billion people worldwide.
  h) You can get TB when somebody with it sneezes or coughs near you.

3 Look at the title of this passage. In your own words describe what it is referring to. Then read the passage.

The new war against TB
The emergence of a devastating drug-resistant strain means that tuberculosis now kills more of us than malaria. Award-winning photographer James Nachtwey travelled all over the world to document the battle against this 'virtually untreatable' and deadliest of diseases.

"Tuberculosis is a shocking disease," explains James Nachtwey, the American war photographer behind these extraordinary images. *"I'm a very experienced journalist. I've seen a lot of terrible things in this world, but witnessing TB is something that affected me as profoundly as anything I saw in Iraq or Afghanistan. My heart went out to the victims and when people see these photographs I hope their hearts will go out to them, too."*

Nachtwey's aim is to bring TB into the 'mass consciousness' in the hope of kick-starting an action campaign that can leverage more funds for aid. *"The problem at the moment is that very few people in the West are even conscious of TB,"* he says. *"The more people are aware of it, the easier it is to raise funds and get sponsorship for research."*

Tuberculosis is one of the oldest diseases known to man and certainly one of the deadliest. Scientists estimate that in the past 400 years TB has killed some two billion people worldwide. It is spread like the common cold or flu by coughing and sneezing, but if it crosses the blood-brain barrier, TB can also cause meningitis, coma and death. *"There are lots of very impressive statistics about TB, but I wanted to put a human face on it,"* said Nachtwey.

As a result of Nachtwey's campaign he has now visited seven countries where TB is widespread, but has also documented new TB hotspots such as Rwanda, Lesotho, Swaziland and Siberia. Also, efforts are being made to negotiate wider access to subsidised drugs and to look at the best timings for medications for patients with TB.

4 Put the following words into the correct gap in the sentences that follow. Read the passage again to check your answers.

> shocking / devastating / sponsorship / profoundly / when /
> impressive / virtually / mass consciousness / witnessing /
> kick-starting / affected

a) Research is being done to find out _____ best to give treatment.

b) The disease can sometimes be treated which means it can _____ but not always be cured.

c) Seeing people suffering from TB affected the photographer _____.

d) By influencing the _____, more than just a few people are being informed.

e) The affects of the disease are very _____ to see. ‖‖▶

f) Many countries are _____ by the disease but until now have got no international help.

g) The campaign needed _____ because not enough was being done about it.

h) _____ suggests something nice or good, but the statistics about TB are not this.

i) You need to have _____ as well as raising funds for a campaign this large.

j) _____ is a very strong word and can have a huge impact on people's lives, as does TB.

k) The photographer found that _____ TB affected him more than other world events.

C Let's speak and listen

You are going to talk about and compare two photographs of weddings.

Before you begin, do the following activities with your partner.

1 Decide if the following words are connected to weddings or not.

bride	reception	mother-in-law	henna
groom	bridesmaids	horseshoe	red
christening	page boys	depressed	trainers
honeymoon	veil	rings	limousine
ceremony	divorce	tuxedo	gifts
cheap	congratulations	teenagers	graduation
university	black	confetti	white

2 Now talk about the following questions with your partner. Complete a copy of the table with your responses.

Question	You	Your partner
Whose wedding have you been to recently?		
What kind of wedding was it, e.g. civil/church/temple, etc.?		
What did the bride and groom wear?		
How was the wedding celebrated?		
Who were the guests?		
Would you say it was a traditional wedding? Why/why not?		
Describe the sort of music played at the wedding.		

3 You are going to turn to page 155 and look at photograph A. Your partner will ask you questions about it and complete the information below. Your partner **must not** look at the photograph.

4 Your partner will now turn to page 156 and look at photograph B. You will ask your partner about it and complete the information below. You **must not** look at the photograph.

Questions Photograph A and B	Answers Photograph A	Answers Photograph B
When was the photo taken? Give reasons for your answer.		
What kind of wedding is it? Give reasons for your answer.		
In which country do you think the wedding took place? Give reasons for your answer.		
How does the photo compare with other wedding photos? Give at least **four** points.		
Describe what the bride is wearing.		
Describe what the groom is wearing.		
What can you understand about the people in the photo?		
How many other people are in the photo? Describe who you think they are.		
Describe how you feel about the photo.		

5 Now look at both of the photographs and talk about them with your partner.

Which photograph do you prefer? Why?

D | Let's read 2

1 Look at the photograph below.

What can you see in the photograph? What do you think the photograph is about? How real do you think the photograph is?

Have you heard the expression 'The camera never lies'? Well, this photograph is not real – it is a fake and the camera did lie. It is called the Cottingley Fairies and was taken in 1917 by two sisters who admitted in 1981 that it was a fake but claimed that they really had seen fairies!

How much do you believe them?

Do you know about any similar photographs?

2 With your partner, talk about the following:
- The different ways the camera can lie.
- How a camera could lie in 1917 and how it can lie today.
- How much technology can influence the way a photograph looks today.
- How much this affects what you believe you see.
- The reasons why a photographer would want to make a picture lie.
- The reasons why the photographers lied about the picture above.

3 You are now going to read a passage about another photograph called the 'Falling Soldier'. Again, there were suggestions that the photo was a fake.

> ### New evidence on mystery of famous 'faked' soldier photo
>
> *The stark black-and-white image of a Spanish Civil War soldier tumbling backwards in the moment of death is one of the best-known – and most controversial – war photographs ever taken.*
>
> *Now, 72 years after the Falling Soldier was first published, an exhibition at the Barbican in London aims to have the last word on whether or not the picture was faked. The photograph made 22-year-old Roberto Capa one of the greatest war photographers.*
>
> *For years arguments have raged as to whether Capa set up the picture or whether he had in fact captured a soldier meeting his violent death. In an age when news took months to travel, it was not unusual for photographers to recreate events.*
>
> *"There have been various theories about whether the soldier was actually shot in battle. Looking at the photos it is clear that it is not the heat of battle. It is likely the soldiers were carrying out an exercise either for Capa or themselves. The images are ordered according to the numbers on the back of the negatives, so it's the best sequence we can put together and from that we can deduce the story."*
>
> *There is no doubt the soldier was shot, however, as it is believed that he died almost instantly from a bullet to the heart.*

Focus on grammar

Coordinating conjunctions – connectives

4 Copy the table on the next page and complete it by putting these conjunctions into the correct category. One has already been done for you.

such as	consequently	similarly	likewise
whether	but	especially	eventually
as … as	then	significantly	too
although	~~for example~~	instead of	because
furthermore	afterwards	in the case of	next
above all	whereas	in particular	in the same way
for instance	and	if	also

To add information	To indicate result	To compare	To contrast
To give examples	**Explaining**	**Sequencing**	**To emphasise**
for example			

5 Find three examples of conjunctions in the passage on page 153.

6 Make complete sentences using one item from each column. Then write the sentences in your book.

You can go to the party …	in particular	…they never go to the theatre.
I like his books …	for instance	…we will finish early today.
You keep going along that road and …	similarly	…you will arrive at the bank.
All children are to wear uniform and …	eventually	…black shoes.
They have to pay …	furthermore	…they enjoy driving there.
They enjoy travelling by plane to Italy and …	whereas	…they have any money or not.
They always go to the cinema …	although	…I don't want you to be late.
I would like to say that all classes will be off and …	whether	…the one about the photographer.

7 Complete each sentence with an appropriate conjunction from Exercise 4.
   a) The cake rises _____ a rising agent was put in the mixture.
   b) I will tell you what I bought for him, _____ you're not to tell him.
   c) I spent a lot of time preparing for the test _____ I know I didn't do well.
   d) You will miss your free time today, and _____ for the rest of the week.
   e) You eat your lunch and _____ you can have an ice-cream.
   f) The girls have brought the right things as _____ have the boys.
   g) 'We will cook something different today _____ Chinese food.'
   h) Numbers have fallen _____ in the younger levels.

Focus on vocabulary

The phrase 'in the heat of the battle' means in the middle of a battle whilst it is being fought.

8 Match the following phrases to their meaning.

Phrase	Meaning
Dicey situation	Get married
Straight from the horse's mouth	Alert, knowledgeable
Hunky-dory	Take a risk
Over the top	Legal
Under the weather	Not well
Tie the knot	All okay
Keep your shirt on	Too much
In the red	Wrong idea or assumption
On the ball	Pass on the responsibility
Above board	Something to be proud of
Clean bill of health	Risky, potentially dangerous
Pass the buck	Directly from the source
Feather in your cap	Stay calm
Bite the bullet	Losing money
Barking up the wrong tree	Healthy

Photographs for Section C
Exercises 3, 4 and 5

Photograph A

Photograph B

E Let's write

Writing a biography

A biography is a written account of the series of events that make up a person's life.

As we saw in Coursebook 2, when writing a biography you should include the following:
- date and place of the person's birth and death
- their life-time accomplishments
- their effect/impact on society or historical significance.

When writing, remember the following:
- keep it interesting for your reader
- start your writing with an interesting statement
- maintain your reader's interest through the main body of your biography by including interesting facts about your subject
- end your biography by summarising your main points
- proofread your essay.

You are going to write a biography of the photographer in this unit – Roberto Capa. Look at the notes in the research section below. They will provide you with the information you need to find out about him, and complete your biography.

F Let's do some research

You are going to research and write about the photographer Roberto Capa. Find out the following about him before you write your biography and make sure you include the points in the writing section above:

- where and when he was born
- the wars he photographed
- his real name and why he changed it
- the reason he changed his identity
- some of his main works
- how, when and where he died
- include a photograph of him and some of his works.

G Let's learn something new

- The word 'camera' comes from Latin and means chamber (room). Thus comes the phrase 'camera obscura' which refers to a dark chamber and was the term used for the first camera – a black box with a lens.
- Colour photography is the mixing of the three primary colours – red, blue and yellow – for all the colours we see.
- Kodak was created by the American, George Eastman, in 1888.

Unit 13 Life then and now

 Let's start

1 Look at the pictures of the two kitchens and talk to your partner about how they are similar and different. Use the prompts to help you.

Prompts	Then (400 years ago)	Now
How the dishes were washed. How food was kept fresh. How food was cooked. How clothes were washed. How food was stored to keep it away from insects, etc. The kind of kitchen utensils that were available. What fuel was used.		

2 What do you think were the advantages and disadvantages of kitchens then and now? Complete a table like the one below to organise your thoughts. The following ideas and example will help you.

	Then		Now	
	Advantages	Disadvantages	Advantages	Disadvantages
Type of food cooked. Type of food bought. How food was cooked. Who the food was cooked by. Your ideas.				Lots of chemicals

3 We have looked at kitchens 400 years ago. Now think about other features of life then – what was life like? Look at the statements below about life 400 years ago and decide if they are true or false.

- Trains had begun transporting people and objects.
- Women could vote in most developed countries.
- People's life expectancy was much lower – at about 35 years.
- Children went to primary and secondary school in most developed countries.
- Streets were lit with oil for the first time.
- There was no sewerage system and dirty water and waste were thrown into the streets.
- New foods and drinks were available, like tea and coffee and bananas and pineapples.
- Doctors had a very limited knowledge of a person's body and anatomy.
- Thousands of people died from the bubonic plague – a disease carried by rats.
- Global warming began because of industrialisation.
- Toothbrushes were used for the first time.
- It was fashionable for men to shave and wear wigs.
- Women wore corsets (a type of underwear) under their dresses, made from wood or whalebone.
- People began eating with forks.
- Glass was first used in windows.
- Houses began to be built not from wood, but stone or brick.

4 Think about your country at the beginning of the 17th century. How different was it from today? What major events were happening then? Share your ideas with your partner and make a list. Then share them with your class. How many different ideas did you think of?

B Let's read 1

'We learn from history that we learn nothing from history.'
George Bernard Shaw – Irish playwright

1 What does the quotation mean? How much do you agree or disagree with it? Give examples to support your answer.

2 Think about events in your lifetime and list them in the appropriate boxes of a table like the one below.

Think about things which have had an impact on your life, e.g. got very low grades in your exams, etc.

An event/s which happened last week:	An event/s which happened last month:	An event/s which happened last year:	An event/s which happened a couple of years ago:	An event/s which happened years ago:

3 With your partner, talk about how some, if any, of the events in your life affect what you do today.

Talk about the following:
- what the event was
- in what way the event was important in your life
- how it influenced/influences actions you made/make as a result
- whether you feel you learn from events that happen in your history or not.

4 We are going to look at events that happen on a wider world scale and see how, if at all, they influence people's behaviour today. First of all, however:
a) match the event with the date
b) put the events into the correct chronological order.

> 44BC 476AD 800AD 1099 1326 1536 1854 1914
> 1929 1939 1945 1972 1994 2002 2005 2008

- Nelson Mandela became President of South Africa.
- The Great Depression.
- Crusaders arrived in Jerusalem.
- Scandinavian explorers, the Vikings, raided and colonised large parts of Europe.
- London bombed by terrorists.
- Nazi Germany invaded Poland.
- First black American president elected.
- Anne Boleyn, second wife of King Henry VIII, was beheaded.
- Western Roman Empire ended.
- World War I began.
- Atomic bomb dropped on Hiroshima and Nagasaki.
- Taliban captured Afghanistan.

- Ottoman Empire founded.
- Crimean War.
- Julius Caesar assassinated.
- Eleven athletes murdered at the Olympic Games.

5 Discuss the following about the world events in Exercise 4:
- Could any be repeated?
- Could any not be repeated? Why?
- Which of the events, if any, do you think we have learnt from?

6 You are now going to read an extract where the writer talks about the subjects you have been discussing.
- **a)** Find how many times the expression 'We learn nothing from history' appears.
- **b)** Find the three groups of people from the passage who also appear in Exercise 4.

Humans have mistreated, beated and eated other humans since history began. They are still doing it, somewhere in the world. We learn nothing from history. Humans have attacked, hacked and racked other humans for money, for honey or just because they think it's funny. They are still doing it, somewhere in the world. We learn nothing from history.

On the other hand we hideous humans may be learning something from horrible history! Take the Romans. People were crucified, juicified and lion-let-loose-ified in ancient Rome. There isn't a lot of that going on in the world today. Why? Because the Romans got a lot of 'horrible' history written about them. People were shocked.

Just as other monstrous people in history have shocked us, from vicious Vikings chopping up harmless old monks to nasty Nazis slaughtering millions of innocent people because they were the wrong race.

When people learn from 'horrible' history then things DO start to change. After the Nazi terrors were defeated, memorials were put up that said simply:

The world is still full of horrible happenings. But what will happen in the future to you, young readers?

7 In the passage above, four sets of three words rhyme with each other – what are they? Which of the words are made-up words and which words are real? Match the meaning or explanation of each word to one of the definitions below.

- vicious animals were let out in the arena to fight with humans to the death
- to laugh at
- to treat badly or wrongly
- nailed to a cross or something similar
- cut into pieces
- sold
- to hit
- beaten up
- do violence to
- have the bones stretched
- to consume
- for some other form of payment

8 The writer uses **alliteration** in the passage. Alliteration is when two or more words begin with the same letters or sounds so that they 'fit' together and make the writing sound more interesting to the reader. An example is the title of the book, *Horrible Histories*. The writer has used words which stress the horrible nature of the people he is talking about.

Find another three examples in the passage.

9 Use alliteration to describe these people, for example, 'rough Romans'.

> Romans   Crusaders   Scandinavians
> Olympians   students   teachers

10 Complete these sentences about the passage.
    a) The writer thinks people are _____.
    b) The writer thinks people have learnt from horrible history because _____.
    c) The writer thinks some people stopped doing horrible things because _____.
    d) The writer still thinks _____.
    e) The writer hopes young people will _____.
    f) The writer _____.

C Let's speak and listen

1 Ask your partner the following questions and make a note of their answers. Then do the same for your partner by answering the questions for them. Don't worry about the final column at the moment.

Question	Your partner's answers	Stefano's answers
a) Is history important to you? Why/why not?		
b) Do you like studying history at school? Why/why not?		
c) What period of history interests you most? Why?		
d) What period of history interests you least? Why?		
e) What period of history would you like to go back to live in? Why?		
f) What do you know about your family's history?		
g) How important do you think it is to know about your family's history? Why/why not?		
h) If you could change one period of history which would it be? Why?		
i) How would you prevent certain events in history happening?		
j) What do you think would happen if history was no longer taught at school?		

2 Now listen to Stefano and make a note of his answers in the final column.

D Let's read 2

At the beginning of this unit we saw a kitchen from 400 years ago.
Now let's look at kitchens during World War II.

ration card	iron
mangle	stove
covered windows	wireless
brown bread	powdered egg
wash board	limited fresh fruit
metal tub	gas lamp

1 a) Match the words to each of the items in the picture.
　 b) Make ten sentences by matching the two parts below to find out
how life was for a war-time child.

This was how the creases were taken …	… themselves in the kitchen and by warming the water by hand.
This was used when shopping …	… the powdered form would be used instead.
Since there was no television …	
Few homes had electricity …	… enemy planes flying overhead could not be guided by the lights in towns and cities and bomb them.
This was used to wash the clothes …	

This was used to squeeze water …	… because the amount of food bought had to be restricted.
This was recommended as …	… so gas had to be used instead.
This was how people cleaned …	… out and it had to be heated on the stove.
Fresh ones were not available so …	… warming the kitchen using coal or wood.
This was used for cooking and …	… available and so it was limited.
Only home-grown produce was …	… by rubbing with soap and water.
This was done every night so that …	… healthier than white in a limited diet.
	… out of clothes just hand-washed.
	… people used this for entertainment and to get the news.

2 Discuss what the period 1939–1945 was like in your country. How can you find out if you don't know? Answer these questions:
- What fresh food was available?
- What could and couldn't people buy?
- How safe was it to live in the cities?
- How much, if any, damage was done to your country?
- How different were people's lives? Give some examples.
- In what way was your country involved in the war?
- How did war affect the lives of children in your country?

Many children in Britain and other countries had to leave cities because they were being bombed by enemy planes and were not safe. Also, the lack of food and facilities made cities a bad place for children to grow up in. You are going to read an extract from a book called *Goodnight Mister Tom*. It is a moving story about a young boy called Willie Beech who goes to stay with an older man called Mister Tom during the war.

3 Quickly read the extract on the following page once and think of four words that you think might describe how:
a) Willie feels
b) Mr Tom feels.

"Yes," said Tom bluntly, on opening the front door. "What d' you want?"

A harassed middle-aged woman in a green coat and felt hat stood on his step. He glanced at the armband on her sleeve. She gave him an awkward smile.

"I'm the billeting officer for this area," she began.

"Oh yes, and what's that got to do wi' me?"

She flushed slightly. "Well, Mr... Mr ..."

"Oakley. Thomas Oakley."

"Ah, thank you, Mr Oakley." She paused and took a deep breath. "Mr Oakley, with the declaration of war imminent ..."

Tom waved his hand. "I know all about that. Git to the point. What d' you want?" He noticed a small boy at her side.

"It's him I've come about," she said. "I'm on my way to your village hall with the others."

"What others?"

She stepped to one side. Behind the large iron gate which stood at the end of the graveyard were a small group of children. Many of them were filthy and very poorly clad. Only a handful had a blazer or coat. They all looked bewildered and exhausted. One tiny dark-haired girl in the front was hanging firmly on to a new teddy-bear.

The woman touched the boy at her side and pushed him forward.

"There's no need to tell me," said Tom. "It's obligatory and it's for the war effort."

"You are entitled to choose your child, I know," began the woman apologetically. "But his mother wants him to be with someone who's religious or near a church. She was quite adamant. Said she would only let him be evacuated if he was near a church. His name's Willie," she finished lamely.

Tom took a second look at the child. The boy was thin and sickly-looking, pale with sandy hair and dull grey eyes.

Tom in contrast was well into his sixties, a healthy, robust, stockily-built man with a head of thick white hair. Although he was of average height, in Willie's eyes he was a towering giant with skin like coarse, wrinkled brown paper and a voice like thunder.

Focus on grammar

Prepositions of place and movement

Prepositions are used to show movement and place:

> The cat is **on** the chair. (place)
>
> There is a cat **on top of** the chair. (place)
>
> The cat jumped **onto** the chair. (movement)

These prepositions refer to the noun, which always follows it.

4 Look at these four examples of prepositions from the passage:

on   at   near   behind

Find them in the passage and in each case say if they show place or movement.

5 Separate the following prepositions into place, movement or both. One has already been done for you.

on	inside	from/to	below
at	outside	away from	between
near	down/up	towards	in
behind	~~next to~~	past	among
into/onto	by	over	opposite
on top of	beside	under	off/on
in front of	across	through	
around	along	above	

Preposition of place	Preposition of movement	Both
next to		

6 Using some of the prepositions, complete the following sentences:
a) As he walked _____ the door he took out his key to open it.
b) He looked _____ to see what sort of day it was to help him decide what to wear.
c) They have decided to build a block of flats _____ our house, so imagine our annoyance.
d) As the head teacher walked _____ the door, the room went quiet.
e) They are building pavements _____ all the roads to make it safer for pedestrians.
f) The windows _____ the sofa are very dirty and need cleaning.
g) He got _____ the bus at the wrong stop and so had to walk much further.
h) There is a supermarket _____ the school which sells very nice fresh sandwiches.

i) He walked _____ the post office without seeing it and so didn't buy his stamps.

j) The train leaves _____ six o'clock so make sure you don't miss it.

k) They walked _____ the school hall quietly and respectfully as they had been told to do.

7 Write four sentences about yourself and your classroom using some of the prepositions, e.g.

'In the morning I walk through the classroom door into the classroom.'

Focus on vocabulary

8 In the extract on page 166 there is a lot of description about different people. Complete a copy of the table below, although not all the boxes can be filled about each person. Don't worry about the final row yet.

	Age	Hair	Clothes	Height	Complexion	Distinctive features	Build
Mister Tom							
Willie							
Woman							
Little girl							
Children							
Other							

9 Now put the following words, used to describe people, in the appropriate column. Some can be used in more than one column. You may need a dictionary to help you.

straight	lanky	beard	gangly
wavy	swarthy	moustache	dull
curly	sallow	receding	plump
20ish	middle-aged	wrinkles	smart
round	dark	grey	elegant
haggard	bald	obese	tiny
scruffy	in their 60s	stout	towering

In this unit you read that Anne Boleyn, who was the second wife of King Henry VIII, was beheaded. If you describe her appearance, it might be like this:

Anne Boleyn was not considered one of the handsomest women of the day because she had a dark complexion which was not fashionable at the time. She was nonetheless moderately pretty. She had an oval-shaped face with a pointed chin, high forehead and long slender neck. One of her strong features was her eyes, which were almost black like her hair. She was of middling stature and carried herself elegantly.

10 Now think of a person in history that you could describe. Find a picture of them and write a description. Use the description of Anne Boleyn to help you.

 Let's write

Character description

How a writer uses language can tell us something of the person's character she or he is describing.

<u>About Mister Tom:</u>

> "Yes," said Tom bluntly, on opening the front door.
> "What d' you want?"
> "Git to the point."

This suggests that the character is abrupt, which might be to hide something of his true self. This, if we read further in the book, is true because he prefers to hide his feelings as a result of the death of his wife, but he is actually a very loving and caring person.

About the woman:

> A harassed middle-aged woman …
> She gave him an awkward smile.
> She paused and took a deep breath.

This suggests that she is not a confident person and is quite shy of men like Mister Tom.

A person's appearance can also tell us something of their character:

> … a healthy, robust, stockily-built man with a head of thick white hair.

This suggests a strong man with a healthy, outdoor life who enjoys good food.

Write the opening to a story where you introduce two characters. Think about the following:
- the dialogue used to portray the characters
- appearance of the people to help portray their character
- behaviour of the people to portray their character.

F Let's do some research

You are going to do some research about a famous historical character of your choice. To do this you will need to do the following:

a) Write a biography of their life.
b) Write a character description using ideas as shown in this unit.
c) Write a description of their appearance using vocabulary learnt in this unit.
d) Include a picture with the biography.
e) Give examples of quotations, etc. to support your idea of this person.

G Let's learn something new

- People in the 1500s only bathed once a year and with the whole family sharing the water!
- Bread was divided so the workers got the burnt bottom bit, the family the middle and the guests got the top – 'the upper crust'.
- People were sometimes buried alive by mistake, so a bell was attached to the person who could then be 'saved by the bell'.

Medicine through the ages

A **Let's start**

1 Look at each of the pictures. What does each one represent? Talk about them with your partner.

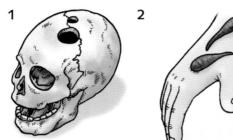 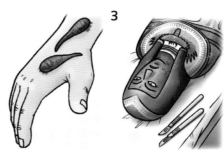 

2 Match each of the pictures with the sentences below.
- A Roman aqueduct brought fresh, clean water to people allowing them to be clean. People recognised that personal hygiene was important.
- The practice of making holes in the skull was called 'trepanning' and was used 10,000 years ago with the idea that by making holes in the skull the evil spirits would be released, so relieving pain.
- Scalpels were used by the Egyptians for the process of mummification or preserving a body when dead.
- Leeches were used by doctors for hundreds of years and as recently as the 1800s. It was believed that a person should be bled when ill because too much blood in the body was the cause of disease.

3 Look at the timeline of medicine over the years on the next page and say if the following statements are true or false.
a) The structure of the human body wasn't understood 900 years ago.
b) Trepanning is one of the earliest forms of medicine.
c) Smallpox has been around for 100 years.
d) People have been living longer in the last 100 years.
e) Mummification was a practice used about 4000 years ago.
f) Hippocrates and Ali al-Husayn Ibn Sina lived about one and a half centuries apart.
g) The use of DNA is one of the most recent advances in medicine.

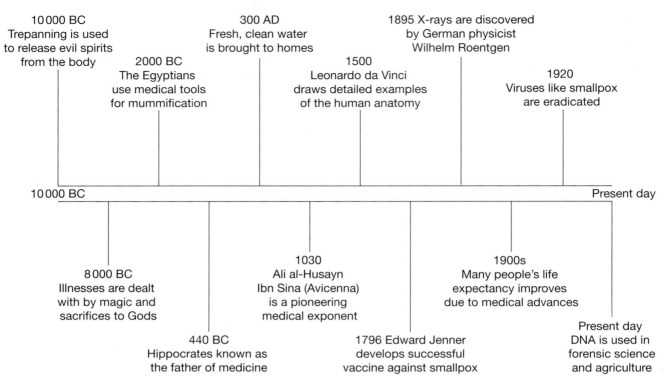

h) X-rays were discovered in the 19th century.

i) Water brought to homes occurred in the 3rd century.

j) About 2000 years ago, the Egyptians had developed in their medical knowledge.

4 Look at the following illnesses and how they were treated in ancient times. Talk to your partner about:

- how they would be treated today
- how much you think the treatments have changed
- in what ways the treatments are better or worse.

Type of illness	Definition	How it used to be treated	How it would be treated today
Cataract	Loss of eye lens clarity	Mixture of tortoise brain and honey applied	
Tooth abscess	Whitish-yellow liquid at base of tooth causing pain	Surgical hole in tooth made	
Psychiatric illness	Mental disorder	Isolation for the patient in a quiet place	
Open wound	An injury due to open skin	Honey or wine and vinegar spread on wound	
Dysentery	Need to go to the toilet	Yellow part of egg eaten	

B Let's read 1

1 With your partner, talk about the different types of medicine and medical treatments that exist/ed, e.g. trepanning. Complete the spider diagram with your ideas.

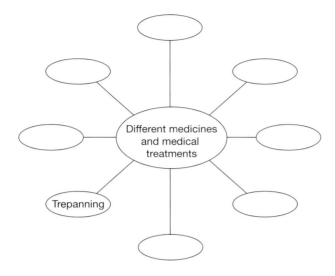

2 How many words did you find? Below are four words connected to different types of medicine and medical treatments. Are they the same as the ones you found? First, you have to work out what the words are. There is a clue to help you.

Clue: The idea of dealing with an illness with symptoms of the same illness.

AYHOOPETHM

Clue: Inserting needles into parts of the body to relieve pain.

PTUCEARCNUU

Clue: Emphasises the body's ability to heal and maintain itself with natural remedies such as herbs and foods.

ANPTOCARITUH

Clue: Involves manipulating (controlling) the bones and muscles.

E O H O S T P T A Y

All of the above are alternative types of medicine – what is alternative medicine? How is alternative medicine different from systems of medicine carried out in your country by conventional doctors at hospitals and clinics?

Have you ever visited a doctor of alternative medicine?

What do you think the benefits are of alternative or conventional medicine? Talk with your partner and complete a copy of the table.

Conventional medicine		Alternative medicine	
Advantages	Disadvantages	Advantages	Disadvantages
More doctors available and trained.			

3 Now, with your partner, talk about the following:
- What is this a picture of?
- What connection do you think it has with medicine?
- In which category of medical treatment does it fit? Why?
- Imagine what it is and make up a story about it.

Now read the passage and check how many of your answers are correct.

The tree of life (and its super fruit)

Baobabs, also known as upside-down trees, produce fruit which are of great medicinal benefit.

The baobab fruit has three times as much vitamin C as an orange, 50 per cent more calcium than spinach and is a plentiful source of antioxidants, those disease-fighting molecules credited with helping reduce the risk of everything from cancer to heart disease. Until recently, this super-fruit was off limits to many consumers, unless they fancied a shopping trip to Africa. But now the baobab fruit has won approval from EU regulators.

Bush legends about the baobab abound. One has it that the god Thora took a dislike to the baobab growing in his garden and promptly chucked it over the wall of paradise; it landed below on earth, upside down but still alive, and continued to grow.

Today, many Africans refer to it as the "Tree of Life", and it's not hard to see why. With a trunk that can grow up to 15m in circumference, a single tree can hold up to 4500 litres of water. Fibres from the bark can be turned into rope and cloth; fresh leaves are often eaten to boost the immune system; and some hollowed-out trunks have been used to provide shelter for as many as 40 people. And then, of course, there's the fruit.

A recent report estimated that the trade in baobab fruit could be worth up to $1 bn a year for African producers, employing more than 2.5 million households across the continent. Also, one advantage to baobab harvesting is that there is no need for fancy start-up equipment. All you need is a pair of hands. And since it is an indigenous plant it is not expected to be as vulnerable to the ravages of climate change that Africa is expected to have to endure over the coming years.

However, there are fears about making Africa's resource sustainable, especially if demand rockets in Europe. "We're blessed with baobab trees, but if this fruit becomes Africa's apple and goes global, which I believe it will, then we need to plant more trees, and now," said Mr Dohse of TreeCrops.

4 Match the following words from the text with a suitable synonym.

Words from the text		**Synonyms**	
medicinal	indigenous	perimeter	lasting
boost	sustainable	healing	recognised
regulators	credited	controllers	ruinous effects
circumference	ravages	protection	gathering
immune	harvesting	native	improve

5 There is a mistake about the passage in each of the sentences below. Find each mistake and correct it.
   a) The bark can be turned into rope and cloth.
   b) The trees are grown upside down.
   c) The baobab tree is an ingenious plant.
   d) More vitamin C is found in an orange than a baobab fruit.
   e) A baobab fruit could be worth up to $1 billion.

f) There is a demand for rockets in Europe.

g) 2.5 million people across the continent will be employed.

h) A shipping trip to Africa is the only way to buy the baobab fruit.

i) The tree has a circumference of 1.5m.

j) The tree is not vulnerable to the ravages of civil war.

C Let's speak and listen

1 An international pharmaceutical company has offered to give $1 billion towards research. You and your partner are members of a select team who have been chosen to select which area of medicine would most benefit from this money. Below are the various options of where the money could be best spent. Together, talk about each of the areas that need research and decide which area should or should not be chosen. You both need to agree on only **one** medical condition that you **both** feel should receive the money.

For each case you need to make notes about why you chose or didn't choose it. Do this in a table like the one below.

	Reasons why chosen	Reasons why not chosen
Cancer		
Heart disease		
Common cold		
Backache		
Mental illness/depression		
Tooth decay		

2 Now listen to Sophia and Dimitris talking about the topic. Add their answers to your table.

D Let's read 2

1 Look at the picture opposite and talk about it with your partner.
- What has happened to the animals?
- What have they been used for?
- Why is this being done to them?

The animals are used for medical research so that medicines can be developed for human illnesses all over the world.

2 Talk to your partner about the negative and the positive aspects of this.

How much do you agree or disagree with animals being used for medical research?

I agree with animals being used for medical research because …	I don't agree with animals being used for medical research because …
	… it is cruel.

3 Look at the following points and decide if each one is a statement in favour of animal testing or against it. Put your answers in a table like this one.

Against animal testing	In favour of animal testing

- It is morally wrong to use animals.
- Nearly everyone has benefited from modern medicine.
- Everyone needs medicine.
- Medicines don't always respond in the same way on animals as on humans.
- The animals are treated cruelly and suffer.
- Animals benefit from modern medicine as well.
- Developments in medicine would not have been possible otherwise.
- Scientists could find other ways to do research if they wanted to.
- Animals have a right to life as much as humans.
- Only specially-bred animals are used, not pets.
- The law protects and controls the animals that are used for testing.

- Rare animals and animals from the wild are used in some countries.
- Animals are looked after and cared for.

4 Complete the table about the text below and then use a dictionary to help you.

Words I know	Words I think I know	Words I don't know

Leading surgeon backs animal testing

One of the country's top brain surgeons has launched an uncompromising attack on the government's decision to set up a centre to promote alternatives to animal experiments.

"There is no substitute for carrying out experiments on animals and it is dishonest to suggest otherwise," said a leading surgeon recently. "If we want to rid ourselves of the scourge of brain disorders such as Parkinson's and Alzheimer's, we must face the fact that we need to carry out animal experiments."

The news of the government's plans was greeted with polite encouragement by senior science officials, cautious optimism from groups such as the RSPCA, and suspicion by anti-vivisectionists.

But many scientists believe the project is misguided and dangerous. "We should be trying to explain to people what the massive benefits are that we get from experiments involving only relatively few animals," said one scientist. He then added "Fewer than 100 macaque monkeys have been used at centres in the US, Britain and France to develop the technique of deep brain stimulation for Parkinson's disease. More than 20 000 patients have benefited from its use and the figure could rise to millions."

Focus on grammar

Modal auxiliary verbs

Modals are special verbs which add certain kinds of meaning connected with certainty or with obligation and freedom to act. They are used before the infinitives of other verbs.

Examples are: *can, could, may, might, will, would, shall, should, must* and *ought*.

5 Find examples of two modals in the text opposite.

6 Look at the sentences below, each of which uses a different modal. Identify the purpose of the modal in each case from those given in the box.

ability	possibility	permission	logical assumption	necessity
advice	criticism	obligation	request	~~offer~~
suggestion	duty	prohibition		

a) **Can** I give you a lift home? – offer
b) She **can** speak French fluently.
c) We **ought** to give some money to charity every month.
d) You **mustn't** smoke in any public buildings.
e) **May** I leave the classroom, Mrs Ivanhoe, please?
f) I **must** change the oil in the car as there is something wrong.
g) It **couldn't** have been him who stole it because he was with me.
h) You **should** go to the cinema tonight, you will enjoy it.
i) You **could** help me carry these bags.
j) Everyone **ought** to bring some food to sell at the bazaar.
k) They **will** be finished soon.
l) **Shall** I pay for them to go on this school trip?
m) **Might** I borrow some of your books, please?

7 Complete the sentences using the prompts given. For example:

(ability) run / 10 km / without stopping

He can run 10 km without stopping.

- (ability) sit at computer / all evening
- (possibility) still be at meeting
- (permission) borrow / pencil
- (logical assumption) be more than 16 years old
- (necessity) go to the toilet
- (advice) not sit in sun
- (criticism) tell the truth
- (obligation) give up smoking
- (request) close the window
- (offer) help carry bags

- (suggestion) start homework earlier
- (duty) do homework each evening
- (prohibition) to wear trousers / school

8 Write an appropriate dialogue, using modal verbs, for each of the situations shown in the pictures.

Focus on vocabulary

Vocabulary related to topic

9 In the text on page 178 you can see some of the following words, which are related to the topic of medicine and animal testing. Find the words which appear in the text and then match each one with its meaning.

experiments	Alzheimer's
encouragement	disorder
disease of brain and nervous system	tests

Parkinson's	disease of older people of the brain
illness	anti-vivisectionists
against animal experiments	stimulation

10 Find out what the underlined words refer to. Use a dictionary or the internet to help you answer the questions.

    a) If a person has vertigo or agrophobia, where don't they like to be?

    b) Angina is used to describe pain in which organ of the body?

    c) Chicken pox is a common illness for which group of people?

    d) Teenagers suffer from acne but what happens to their faces?

    e) A paediatrician looks after which group of people?

    f) How is constipation affected by water and fruit?

    g) A chiropractor would help which part of your body?

    h) When you have food poisoning you vomit – what happens to the food?

    i) If you have a simple fracture, is your bone broken or not?

    j) If your skin had some kind of disease, would you go to a dermatologist?

    k) The funny bone is a bone in which part of your body?

    l) The triceps are what and in what part of the body?

    m) The liver is an organ in the body and deals with what?

    n) Malaria is a disease many children still die from, but which insect carries it?

    o) If a woman has morning sickness, what does it suggest about her?

E Let's write

Formal writing

Look at the text in 'Let's read 2' on page 178 and answer the following questions.

- Who has it been written for?
- Where would you expect to find a piece of writing like this?
- Would you say it is an informal or formal piece of writing? Why?

Formal writing is for an audience unknown to you, and which you want to keep a distance from because of the environment, e.g. a business situation, talking to a head teacher, presenting a speech at a formal gathering, etc.

1 Find examples of the following in the passage from 'Let's read 2', which give it a formal tone.
- Uses complex (not simple) sentences.
- Uses technical words.
- Uses formal vocabulary.
- Uses the passive.
- Uses an impersonal voice – not the first person.
- Uses polite language.
- Has a formal tone.
- Leaves a line between paragraphs.
- Uses formal connectives.

2 Think about other places where informal or formal language would be appropriate, and complete a table with your ideas.

Formal language	Informal language
At school towards the head teacher and teachers.	

3 You are going to write a letter based on the decisions you made in Section C Exercise 1 about where money should be invested. Write the letter to include the points given to you in Exercise 1 above and the guidance below.

Your full postal address
Date
Address the person you are writing to as either: *Dear Sir* or *Dear Madam* or *Dear Sir/Madam*
If you know the name of the person, then write it in full, e.g.
Dear Mr Smith

Introductory paragraph: Explain briefly the reason you are writing.
Main body: Logical sequence of your points.
Last paragraph: A conclusion of what you have said in the letter.

End the letter:
Yours faithfully if you started the letter using Sir/Madam

or
Yours sincerely if you used their name.

Sign your name.
Print your name in full with your title, e.g. Miss/Mr, etc.

Let's do some research

With your partner think about some of the most amazing medical discoveries of our time. Choose one that you would like to find out about. Prepare to do some research on it and to present it to your teacher.

Think about some of the following points:
- The name of it and where it comes from.
- Who discovered it and how.
- When and where it was discovered.
- The effects the discovery has had.
- Whether animals are used to develop the medicine.
- How beneficial the discovery has been on modern medicine.
- How accessible the medicine is for everybody and who it is beneficial for.

Let's learn something new

- Tomato ketchup was sold as a medicine in the 1830s.
- The first owner of the Marlboro Company died of lung cancer.
- If a surgeon in Ancient Egypt lost a patient (they died) while performing an operation, his hands were cut off!

Unit 15 Up, up and away!

A **Let's start**

1 Look at these six sentences about one of man's first attempts at flying. Put them into the correct time order to create the story.

  a) Icarus' father warned him against flying too high near the sun but unfortunately Icarus, who was so ecstatic about flying, forgot his father's warning and flew near the sun.

  b) The wax that attached the feathers to the wooden frame melted and Icarus plunged to his death.

  c) They attempted to escape and in order to do this made some wings from a wooden frame to which they attached leaves with wax.

  d) This dream became reality in the early 20th century.

  e) This story, written thousands of years ago, shows that man's desire to fly has always been a dream.

  f) Icarus and his father Daedalus were imprisoned by King Minos on the island of Crete in Greece.

2 What can you find out about how aeroplanes have developed since the early 20th century?

Talk about the following with your partner.
- The similarities and differences between how planes were at the beginning of the 20th century and now.
- The reasons why you think aeroplanes have changed so much over the years.
- What different materials planes (then and now) are made from and the purposes they have been built for.
- The speed and altitude (height) that modern planes can fly at compared with planes in the past.
- The manoeuvres that planes could do and the manoeuvres they're capable of now.

3 Talk about the following with your partner and make a note of your answers.

Questions	Your answers	Your partner's answers
Have you ever flown?		
What are the best things about flying?		
What are the worst things about flying?		
Would you like to fly like a bird? What bird would you choose to be? Why?		
If you had the choice, where would you fly to now?		
How safe do you think it is to fly?		
Would you rather fly or take some other form of transport? Why?		
How realistic do you think it is that people will fly to the Moon?		
How much do you think aeroplanes add to global warming?		
Do you think the increase in the use of aeroplanes for the tourist industry is a good or bad thing? How?		
What is the future of aeroplanes?		

B Let's read 1

1 What can fly? Make a list.

Find eight different types of aircraft in the word circle below and check your answers:

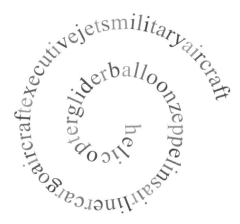

2 How much do you know about the different types of aircraft and how they have changed over the years? Do the following quiz with your partner and say if the following are true or false.

a) The Wright Brothers made the first powered aeroplane flight in history.
b) Amelia Earhart was one of the first women to fly.
c) Aeroplanes can travel faster than the speed of sound.
d) The Zeppelin was a type of airship in 1900.
e) A powerful jet engine can travel as fast as 3200km/h.
f) The words 'airplane' and 'aeroplane' are the same thing.
g) More than 100 billion people pass through the world's airports each year.
h) 1000 aeroplanes can take off in any one day at an airport.
i) You must have a passport if you want to travel internationally.
j) Aeroplanes fly above the clouds to avoid bad weather.
k) The first war to use aircraft was World War II.
l) People flew in balloons and airships before aeroplanes were invented.

3 The Hindenburg was a prototype flying vehicle. Do you know anything about it? With your partner, talk about what you think is happening in the picture.

4 Now make sentences using the text in the box below to find out more about the Hindenburg.

The Hindenburg was a German …	… the fire started.
It was the largest …	… the Hindenburg caught fire and exploded.
It was longer than …	… one of the first eyewitness accounts to be broadcast on radio.
It was fuelled by …	… Europe and the United States.
The Hindenburg travelled between …	… of transport after the accident.
On the 6 May 1937 …	… of the Zeppelins built in the 1930s.
Fire was seen to start and then …	… 36 people were killed in the accident.
It was attempting to dock and …	… there was an explosion.
People lost confidence in this form …	… airship and a first form of public transport.
There are many theories on how …	… flammable hydrogen.
Commentary on the accident was …	… 244 metres.

5 You are going to read an account of the Hindenburg disaster in the report below. But before you do that, look at the following words – have they been spelt correctly?

tremendos   alltitude   assissting   recaled

Find the words in the report below and check to see if you were correct.

Robert Buchanan lived in Toms River, USA as a young man and was hired to work on the ground crew assisting in landing and tethering the huge lighter-than-air airships. Acting like human anchors, crewmen on the ground grabbed ropes and held the ship in place while a larger rope was winched at the mooring mast.

Buchanan recalled on the fateful day that the Hindenburg came in at an altitude higher than it normally did, and it was the extra height that gave all but one of the ground crew time to scramble from beneath the falling and burning monster. Buchanan recalled with sadness the one crew member who tripped on the mooring mast tracks and was burned by the falling wreckage.

Buchanan said that he first knew something was wrong when the number one engine revved up and sparks and flame spewed from the exhaust. Almost instantly, the ship was afire, and the heat was tremendous. Buchanan lamented that no one investigating the cause of the crash accepted his account of the flaming engine and included it among the causes of the crash.

Buchanan credits the heavy sweater he wore that day, soaking wet from rain, with keeping the heat from burning him as the hydrogen-fed fire burned. And while he is not certain, Buchanan believes that he is the last surviving member of the ground crew on that fateful day.

6 Answer the questions on the report above. Your teacher will help you with any difficult words, and you can use a dictionary.
a) What job did Buchanan have in 1937?
b) Describe in your own words how the Hindenburg usually docked.
c) What circumstance gave some ground crew the chance of survival?
d) Why did the one ground crewman not survive?
e) What was not accepted from Buchanan?
f) What does Buchanan believe saved him?
g) How many people are still alive who witnessed the event?
h) Why was the fire on the Hindenburg so strong?

C Let's speak and listen

1 How much do you know about aeroplanes? Where does the captain sit? What does the aeroplane land on?

With your partner, match the words to the picture of the aeroplane below.

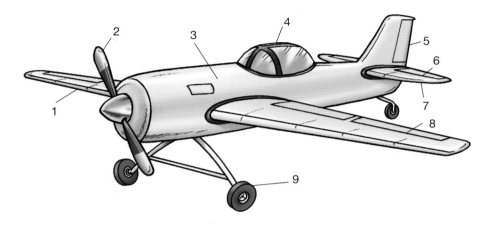

a) rudder	d) elevator	g) propeller
b) wings	e) fuselage	h) stabilisers
c) cockpit	f) flaps	i) wheels

2 But what does each part do? Again with your partner, decide what each part does. Then match the purpose with the number.

a)	Landing gear.
b)	Help keeps an aircraft steady and moves it to the left and right.
c)	Moves to pitch the aircraft up or down.
d)	Body of the aircraft that has space for baggage and seats.
e)	Where the controls are located and where the pilot sits.
f)	Balances the aircraft.
g)	Turning blades that pull the aircraft through the air.
h)	Act as brakes on landing and create lift for take off.
i)	Lift and support for weight of aircraft and contain fuel tanks.

Now listen to check that you got the answers correct.

D Let's read 2

1 What are the following and what does each one refer to?

The Few		An Ace	510	2927 and 90	British, Australian, Canadian, South African, New Zealander
1700	'Never was so much owed by so many to so few.'	Battle of Britain	RAF	1940	

2 Match each of the above to one of the sentences below.
- Spitfire pilot and leading Ace killed in 1941.
- This was the first battle fought solely by the air force and helped stop Britain being invaded.
- Number of RAF Spitfire fighters and other airmen killed in the war.
- Royal Air Force.
- Quotation by Winston Churchill and where the fighters got their name.
- Air force pilot with confirmed five hits.
- Main nationalities of men who were RAF fighters.
- A war memorial (in memory of those who died).
- Describes the airmen who flew Spitfires and other planes, and helped end the war.
- The number of Spitfire and other aircraft pilots in World War II and roughly the number still alive today.
- The number of German aircraft shot down by Spitfires and other planes.
- The year the Battle of Britain was fought.

3 Over the years Spitfires and their pilots have been romanticised, and films, books and songs have been written about them.

With your partner talk about the following.
- Why the idea of a Spitfire and its pilots has been romanticised so much.
- What do you think about the idea of romanticising something like a Spitfire?
- Do you think the pilots of Spitfires were heroes? Why/why not?
- Would you like to have been a Spitfire pilot? Why/why not?
- Do you think countries should remember what the Spitfire pilots did and build memorials for them? Why/why not?

4 You are going to read an obituary (biography of somebody who has recently died) about a man who was a Spitfire pilot. First of all match the words and their synonyms in the box below, then read the extract to help you understand the meanings.

nickname	infamous	notorious
severing	exploits	adventures
investigation	squadron	cutting off
bailed out	sobriquet	reconnaissance
team	escaped	

5 Look at the title of the extract and find out what the abbreviations stand for.

Sqn Ldr Frank Day: 'Fearless' Spitfire pilot

Frank Day, who earned the sobriquet "Fearless" for his exploits as a Spitfire pilot in the Second World War, seldom referred to the fact that he was imprisoned in a notorious prisoner-of-war camp from 1942 to 1945.

Day was the son of a successful wine merchant in the City of London and the overpowering ambition of his youth was to qualify as a pilot in the RAF, which was achieved in his early twenties.

In 1942, Day was sent on a photo-reconnaissance flight over the island of Crete, during which he was attacked by a squadron of Messerschmidt 109s (German equivalent to the Spitfire). The gunfire shattered his control column, severing his right thumb and wounding him in the leg. He bailed out and was in the sea for 24 hours. He was rescued, eventually, by Italians stationed on the island who took him to the German hospital in Heraklion, Greece, and later to a prisoner-of-war camp. Here he was interviewed by the escape committee, who didn't rate his chances of joining them because of his injured leg and missing thumb. He was employed instead as one of 20 "penguins" who stored the earth from the tunnels in their trousers and scattered it casually in the prison grounds. These events were described in a book by Paul Brickhill and in the movie 'The Great Escape', starring Steve McQueen. Most of the men who managed to dig their way to freedom were rounded up by the Nazis and shot.

Frank, who left the RAF as a squadron leader, found post-war employment in a pharmaceutical company where he later ended up as the managing director. Although he was profoundly moved by the deaths of his comrades in the camp, and the horrific sights he had witnessed, there was no bitterness in his nature.

Focus on grammar

Nouns

6 Match each description with a suitable noun example.

Descriptions	Noun examples
A countable noun	family
An uncountable noun	news
The plural form of the countable noun	men
The articles used with a countable noun	boy
The article used before a vowel	belief
The article used before a consonant	frying pan
The article used when referring to a specific noun	an
The article used when referring generally to a noun	sheep
A countable plural noun	police
A countable noun that looks singular but is plural	sand
A noun that looks plural but is not	scissors
A group/collective noun	a/an
A noun that doesn't change in the singular or plural form	Peter
An irregular plural noun	a
A compound noun	boys
An abstract noun	painters
A concrete noun	the
A proper noun	a/an

7 Find the following in the extract about the Spitfire pilot.

- Two proper nouns
- An abstract noun
- Two group/collective nouns
- An article and its specific noun
- A compound noun
- A concrete noun
- A noun that doesn't change in the singular or plural form
- A countable noun

8 Match the two halves:

A squadron of …	… companies.
A committee of …	… rubbish.
A delegation of …	… bees.
A conglomerate of …	… academics.
A swarm of …	… fighters.
A company of …	… prisoners.
A heap of …	… eggs.
A batch of …	… senators.

9 Think of six countable nouns or noun phrases to fit into each of the uncountable noun categories below. The example in each category will help you.

	The weather	The news	Food	The military
1	The sun	The newsreader	A loaf of bread	A soldier
2				
3				
4				
5				
6				
7				

Focus on vocabulary

Phrasal verbs

A phrasal verb is a verb which combines with another word or words, for example, 'show up', 'get on with'. In this unit we will only look at some of the more common ones. Some phrasal verbs need to be separated, e.g. ask out = He <u>asked</u> me <u>out</u> to dinner, while others do not: He <u>showed</u> <u>up</u> on time.

There are two examples in the extract above:

> Bailed out = escaped.
>
> Rounded up = formed into a controllable group.

10 Match the phrasal verb with its meaning and then complete the sentences on the following page using the correct one.

Phrasal verb	Meaning
blow up	discover
break down	take care of
call on	visit
care for	be careful
fill in	make quiet
find out	complete
get up	distribute
give out	arrange
hand in	solve
hold on	discard
keep out	explode
look after	nurse somebody
pass away	rise
put down	die
run out (of)	remove
set up	not have enough of something
shut up	insult or say bad things about
take off	submit
throw out	stop working properly
watch out	prevent from entering
work out	wait

a) You should order some more paper as again we have _____ .

b) You should try and _____ the maths by yourself instead of always asking someone.

c) Could I ask you to _____ my cats while I am away and feed them, please.

d) The car _____ on the motorway and she was left stranded.

e) _____ tightly as otherwise you will fall over.

f) You must _____ all your essays by the dates given by your teacher.

g) You shouldn't _____ all your paper, you should recycle it.

h) You should _____ your grandma more often as she loves to see you.

i) Unfortunately, his grandfather _____ last week and he was at his funeral.

j) If you don't _____ now, I'm going to ask the teacher to move you.

E Let's write

Bias

In writing, **bias** is when the writer allows their feelings about something to affect their writing, and is subjective. If a piece of writing is **unbiased** then it gives a fair and balanced view of the facts and is objective.

The extract 'Sqn Ldr Frank Day: "Fearless" Spitfire pilot' is fairly biased because it is an obituary. Obituaries usually talk about the person who has died in a positive and affectionate way.

There are different ways that bias can be used in writing:

a) By using emotive language, i.e. words that affect the reader's emotions, e.g.

'The crowds were **rowdy**.' Aggressive and noisy.

'The crowds were **noisy**.' Just noisy.

'The food was **delicious**.' Much more than just nice.

'The food was **nice**.' Just nice.

b) By selection – leaving out details which might have a negative impact on the reader.

c) By exaggeration – making more of an issue than necessary.

d) By underplaying – making less of an issue than what really occurred.

Examples for each of the above from the extract on pages 190–191 are as follows:

a) *... who earned the sobriquet 'Fearless' ...*
This opening to the extract immediately endears the reader to the character being written about.

b) There is no mention of how many men might have been killed by Sqn Ldr Frank Day.

c) The use of words like 'notorious' and 'exploits' makes the story exciting and gives the idea of his participation in the war as being one of adventure, drawing parallels with a famous film.

d) *... there was no bitterness in his nature.*
Plays down any feelings he might have had against the enemy.

1 Think about a person or event that stirs your emotions and write a biased account of it. Write about 150 words.

2 Rewrite the account but make it more objective and unbiased.

F Let's do some research

We have been looking at aircraft and used that as a base to study history, but many other things have changed over the years. Think about an area that interests you and one that has been through many changes since the early 20th century, for example, cars, fashion, school, etc. Do some research on the topic of your choice and record the many changes that have occurred. Use pictures to show the changes. Talk about the impact that these changes have brought about.

G Let's learn something new

- Dogs were used in World War II by strapping explosives to their backs and training them to crawl under tanks. The tanks (and the dogs!) were destroyed.
- The population in Hiroshima in 1945, where the first atomic bomb was dropped, was 255 000.
- The heaviest tank in World War II, the German Maus II, was 193 tons (about 192 000 kilos).

The appliance of science

A Let's start

1 Look at the pictures of the following objects and with your partner guess what each of them is.

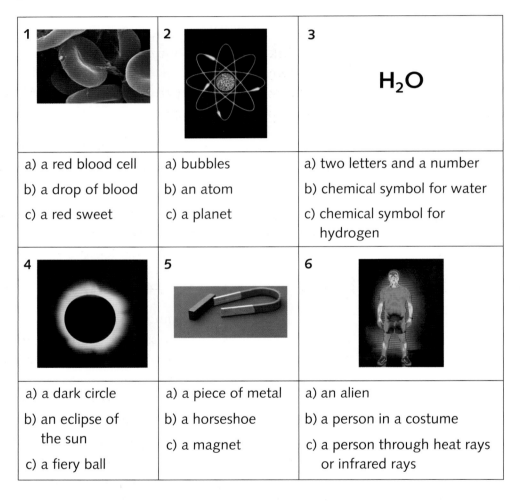

1	2	3
		H_2O
a) a red blood cell	a) bubbles	a) two letters and a number
b) a drop of blood	b) an atom	b) chemical symbol for water
c) a red sweet	c) a planet	c) chemical symbol for hydrogen

4	5	6
a) a dark circle	a) a piece of metal	a) an alien
b) an eclipse of the sun	b) a horseshoe	b) a person in a costume
c) a fiery ball	c) a magnet	c) a person through heat rays or infrared rays

2 All the pictures above are connected to science – but what is science? Complete the definition by piecing the sentences below and on the next page together, then putting them in the correct order.

The word 'science' …

… observable physical evidence through the areas of …

Science is where humans attempt …

This is done through the study of …

… comes from the Latin meaning 'knowledge'.

… to discover and understand better how the natural world works.

… chemistry, physics, biology, astronomy, etc.

3 Talk about the following with your partner.
  a) What science subjects do you study at school?
  b) Do you enjoy science? Why/why not?
  c) How important is it to learn about science? Why?
  d) Why is science becoming less popular at school?
  e) Could science be taught in a different way? How?
  f) What kind of people enjoy science?
  g) Think of at least four discoveries that have been made through science.
  h) It is said that 'Science is the power of Man'. What is meant by this and do you agree?

4 How much do you know about science? From the words in the box, choose the correct one to write in front of the following descriptions.

An eclipse	24 hours	Migrating
Vertebrates	Evaporation	Viruses
Tides	A radio telescope	Gravity
A vacuum	Elements	Sunspots
The Solar System	The tongue	Botany

  a) _____ is the scientific study of plants.
  b) _____ are tiny parasites that can't be seen with an ordinary microscope but cause many diseases.
  c) _____ are living things that all have a backbone.
  d) _____ is an empty space.
  e) _____ can be solid, liquid or gas and all material things on Earth are made up by one or more of these.
  f) _____ are the movement of water that are influenced by the Moon.
  g) _____ is the number of hours in a day according to Man but not Nature.
  h) _____ is a sun and all the bodies around it that are controlled by gravity.
  i) _____ is a sort of giant 'eye' that sees by radio waves sent out from the stars.
  j) _____ is when the Sun, Earth or Moon passes in front of one of the others and hides it.

k) _____ is the force that pulls every object in the universe towards others.

l) _____ is the process where a liquid changes into gas or vapour.

m) _____ birds are those that fly to warmer climates to improve their food and water supply.

n) _____ are tremendous whirls of electrical matter that come bursting out of the interior of the sun in pairs.

o) _____ is an organ and muscle in the body that helps us speak and eat.

B Let's read 1

1 Look at the country shaded orange on the map. Choose the correct answers:

1 This country is called:	2 It is located in:	3 It has a:	4 It is the _____ nation in its area.
a) Singapore b) Ireland c) Qatar	a) Europe b) America c) Asia	a) tiger economy b) mouse economy c) elephant economy	a) smallest b) largest c) weakest
10 It is: a) not serious about science b) serious about the arts c) serious about science	MALAYSIA INDONESIA		5 In 2007 its growth rate was: a) 0.5% b) –3% c) 7.6%
9 Biopolis and Fusionopolis are names given to: a) new towns b) Greek scientists c) research and science centres	8 The government is spending lots of money: a) on science and new ideas b) on their history c) on poverty	7 It spends about _____ on science: a) $3000 b) $3.1 billion c) $3.1 million	6 It is the world's: a) 44th largest economy b) 44th smallest economy c) 2nd largest economy

We can see that Singapore has a great interest in science. This is also shown in how science is taught in schools.

2 Look at the information below and note that Singapore ranks first in its teaching of science in schools. Look at the other countries – where do you think they go in the rankings?

Discuss with your partner. Then talk about where you think your country would go in the rankings if it is not in the list already.

Ranking in world	Countries in order	Other countries
1st	Singapore	Argentina
2nd		Dubai
3rd		Finland
4th		India
15th		Japan
30th		Singapore
54th		Taiwan
61st		United Kingdom

3 Now talk about the following:
- Why do you think science is such an important subject in Singapore?
- What advantages do you think Singaporeans will have in the future?
- What are the disadvantages of science being ranked so high at school?
- How much do you think your country could learn from Singapore?
- Give reasons why you placed your country in the rankings where you did.

4 You are going to read about the teaching of science at a school in Britain. First skim the text to find out how many times the word **science** is used – is it six or seven times?

The appliance of science

A British high school is doing its bit to inspire a new generation of scientists.

Science may involve balancing chemical equations and examining the life cycle of a caterpillar but it's also about space travel, the Big Bang and amazing chemical experiments. That's the message being sent out to the school's 1760 pupils amid a national downturn in interest in science.

According to a new national poll, more than half of nine-year olds are turned off by Physics, Chemistry and Biology. The older they become, the less inspired they are. In the long term this lack of interest in the subjects may damage the country's economy, as there simply won't be enough scientists in the workforce.

Money was invested in the school with the result that facilities and equipment were improved as well as attitudes. "We have a real focus to keep as much practical work as possible. Last year we started a new course called science in the workplace. A third of that course is about forensics, looking at things like fingerprinting. The students absolutely love doing things like that," said the assistant head teacher. She continued: "They do fun activities that they maybe wouldn't be able to do in normal lessons, like mixing chemicals to make rockets or doing astronomy for the first time. We now have an astronomy club and an ecology club with an ecology area in the school grounds where the kids look at animals and species, green issues and an organic garden. The trick is to make science relevant to the students, and if you can do that, it's much easier to capture their imaginations. The results are there for all to see because while single science is compulsory in most secondary schools, many of the students at our school are opting to study triple science and demand filled two classrooms last year!"

This shining example is a far cry from the national picture. According to a study done of 4000 children aged 9–14, youngsters find the subject less inspiring and relevant to their lives as they move from primary to secondary school.

5 Answer the following questions about the passage above.

a) List four things that the school does to encourage students to take up science.

b) Say what the following numbers refer to: 4000; 9–14; 1760.

c) What are the two negative points of children not studying science at school?

d) Find three subjects connected to science in the passage.

e) Find synonyms for the following: motivate; age group; pertinent.

f) Find antonyms for the following: unremarkable; optional; useless.

C Let's speak and listen

1 Look at the following words and, with your partner, decide if they are connected to Biology, Chemistry or Physics. Write your decisions in a table like the one below. One answer has been done for you.

the rock cycle	sound	reproduction
acids	elements	chemical reactions
health and disease	diet and digestion	electricity
space	green plants	~~movement~~
life processes	compounds	
light	magnetism	

Biology	Chemistry	Physics
movement		

2 To each of the words above, match the pair of related words below. For example:

movement – muscles and skeleton

vitamins and carbohydrates	the solar system and gravitational forces
male and female	grains and minerals
North pole and South pole	liquid and gases
lead and gold	Sun and infrared
smoking and antibiotics	water and carbon dioxide
~~muscles and skeleton~~	a candle burning and iron rusting
positive and negative	echo and pitch
growth and respiration	
vinegar and lemons	

3 Listen and check your answers.

D Let's read 2

1 Science, when applied, can dramatically change and improve many features of our society. The Nobel Prize is an international and well-known award that recognises an individual's contribution to society. Do you know which areas it awards prizes for? It is awarded individually in each of the following six areas.

Physics	Chemistry	Physiology and Medicine
Peace	Literature	Economics

2 Match the phrases to find out more about the Nobel Prize.

It is an international award given …	… the Red Cross
It is awarded in the areas of …	… 10 December
It was named after and paid for by …	… Alfred Nobel the Swedish inventor in 1833
He developed dynamite to be used …	… Physics
The first prize was awarded in …	… to fund the work of the recipient
It was awarded to …	… Peace
It was also awarded for Peace to …	… Literature
They were founders of …	… each year
Others famous people who were awarded the Nobel prize were Ernest Hemingway for …	… 1901
Einstein for … and Martin Luther King Jr. for …	… a medal and a cheque for over $1 million
It is awarded each year by the …	… King of Sweden
on …	… Henry Dunant and Frédéric Passy
The prize is …	… in construction and not warfare
This cheque is to be used …	… Wilhelm Röntgen in Physics for the invention of X-rays
	… Physics, Chemistry, Physiology and Medicine, Peace, Literature and Economics

3 On page 204 are pictures of two objects that have been developed with the appliance of science – The Porsche 911 Turbo and the Smart Heart. Do you think the people who invented and developed these or the Spitfire should receive a Nobel Prize in their areas? Why/why not?

4 With your partner list one invention, area or person that you think should get the Nobel Prize in each of the areas, and give reasons for your choices. Use a table like the one opposite.

	Name of person/ invention, etc.	What they developed	Reasons why chosen
Physics			
Chemistry			
Physiology and Medicine			
Peace			
Literature			
Economics			

5 Now talk about the following with your partner.

The Porsche 911 Turbo	A Smart Heart

a) Explain the reasons **why** each of the above was developed.

b) From where, do you think, was the financing for each obtained?

c) Is one more important than the other? Why?

d) Can you think of two areas, mechanical and physical, that you think should benefit more from the appliance of science?

e) Can you think how either of the objects above will assist mankind in the future?

6 Below are five sentences about the car and five about the heart, but they are all mixed up. The order remains the same. Put them under the correct heading in a copy of the table below.

The complex organ that is within science's grasp	The appliance of science

a) A mechanical heart has been the dream of surgeons for many years.

b) The new model will cost very close to $161 620, more if you order a set of ceramic brakes.

c) With the increasing burden of heart disease and a chronic shortage of donor organs, it is cheering to think that science could design a prosthetic organ capable of reproducing the essential functions of the body's main pump.

d) The latest device is an exciting fusion of titanium, animal tissue and aeronautical technology.

e) As usual, there seems to be no shortage of people prepared to put their money down, even though they have no idea what the special features might be.

f) We are still a long way from cheap, spare parts that could make us as good as new.

g) Patients with the latest fully implantable model, Abicor, can expect to live up to five months after surgery – twice as long as they could have expected without it.

h) Nobody could ignore the simply ballistic acceleration or an engine response so sharp it almost takes you by surprise in the lower gears.

i) It is indeed an impressive piece of engineering and it only sounds expensive until you look at the competition and the amount of technical excellence packed into a small space.

j) A more immediate way to save lives, however, would be for more people to carry a donor card.

Focus on grammar

Prepositions and verbs

Certain verbs are followed by particular prepositions. Examples are:

Verb	Preposition
laugh	at
search	for

7 Find two more examples from the passage on page 200.

8 Look at the list of verbs on the left-hand side below. Which prepositions can each verb combine with? One has been done for you. Copy and complete the table.

	into	for	of	about	after	with	on	to	at
talk				✓					
laugh									
agree									
pay									
ask									
look									
search									
work									

9 Michael is confused about which preposition to use and has used the wrong ones. Help him to find the right ones.

a) You should look after more information for your project.
b) He should ask with it if he wants something.
c) Can you look at that book you lost please?
d) Don't talk into them as they are very unfriendly.
e) They have searched to a new car for months now but nothing.
f) They get on very well and always laugh about each other.
g) When you go to school today, ask what happened of Sally Ann.
h) Did you agree of each other what film to see?
i) Don't look on me like that, I don't like it!
j) They work at each other as well as live together!

If we use a preposition and then a verb, we always use the -ing form of the verb. Examples are:

- I found the road without using a map.
- I thanked him for lending me the book.
- After having a cup of tea she felt better.

10 Complete each of the sentences using one of the following prepositions and one of the verbs in the -ing form.

after	for	study	ask
before	of	phone	work
by	about	get	avoid
without	in	arrive	win

a) He apologised _____ _____ late yet again!
b) Going out _____ _____ wet is impossible in this weather.
c) _____ _____ her you are not managing to sort out the argument.
d) You can have this cake _____ _____ and saying 'sorry'.
e) You should have something to eat _____ _____ as you will feel more rested.
f) I'm tired _____ _____ all the time.
g) I thought _____ _____ for a salary increase. What do you think?
h) He has never succeeded _____ _____ any prizes for his team.

Focus on vocabulary

The adjective, the person, the verb, the adverb and the noun

Look at the different parts of speech for some words from this unit.

The adjective	The person	The verb	The adverb	The noun
mechanical	mechanic	mechanise	mechanically	machine
surgical	surgeon	–	surgically	surgery
technical	technician	–	technically	technology
–	carrier	carry	–	carrier
full	–	–	fully	fullness

11 Look back through the unit and write down any words from the table that you can find.

12 Now copy and complete the table below in the same way as the one above.

The adjective	The person	The verb	The adverb	The noun
interesting				
	engineer			
		walk		
			slowly	
				employment

13 Identify the part of speech for each of the coloured words in the following sentences.
   a) The personnel of the personnel department asked him very personal questions.
   b) The managers of the management team managed the children very well.
   c) The cook cooked the meat until it was overcooked.
   d) The English spoke such bad English that I had to ask them to repeat it.
   e) The ambitiousness of the most ambitious in the class made my ambitions look non-ambitious.
   f) The inventions of the inventor had been invented before so they were not new inventions.

E Let's write

Charts, graphs and tables

In Section B Exercise 2, we saw information about science taught in different countries. A chart, graph or table can be used in writing to show more clearly the relationship between data and information. There are four main types:

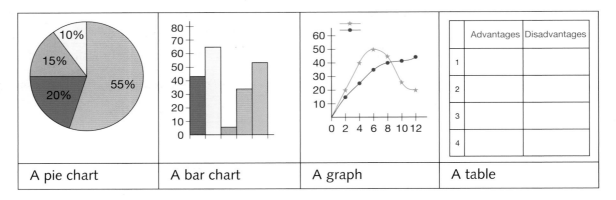

| A pie chart | A bar chart | A graph | A table |

1 Say if the following are true or false.
   a) A pie chart is divided into parts which normally show percentages.
   b) A bar chart is divided into columns.
   c) A graph usually shows information with a line.
   d) A graph is made up of two lines called axes.
   e) The bottom line is the vertical axis and the other is the horizontal axis.
   f) The different axes have different information.
   g) A table has the information arranged in columns and rows.
   h) A table only uses numbers to inform.

2 Choose the correct words to describe the direction of the arrows. One has been done for you.

plunge	rise	soar	plummet
increase	hold steady	flatten out	drop
fluctuate	recover	bounce back	climb
decrease	~~decline~~	reverse	level off

Decline						

Remember there are different ways that the language in this word box can be used, depending on the part of speech used. We can use the word 'decline' in the following way to talk about the table in Section B Exercise 2:

- There was *a steady decline* [a noun] in the level of science taught in schools between Singapore and Argentina.
- The levels taught in schools between Singapore and Argentina *declined steadily* [a verb].

3 Look at the information below from Section B Exercise 2 about science taught in schools. Transfer the information and complete a table with it. Then do the same but in graph form.

4 Write a paragraph describing the following information using the language in Exercise 2. Write about 120 words.

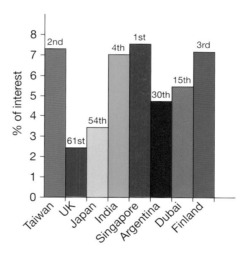

 Let's do some research

You are going to find out the following information from your school colleagues and transfer the information so that it is shown clearly in either a chart, graph or table.

You may choose one or more of the following topics to do research on and you may need your teacher to help you:

- The numbers who enjoy studying sciences: boys and girls/the different science subjects.
- Those who would consider doing science at university/college and the areas they would specialise in.
- The most popular subjects studied at school other than sciences.
- School grades achieved in the different sciences and how they compare.

G Let's learn something new

- About four million different chemicals have been made by chemists.
- Diamonds are found about 200 km under the Earth!
- A space shuttle costs about $1 billion per mission and is built to do 100 missions in its lifetime.

A Let's start

1 Look at the following pictures. What can you say about them? What has each one got that is similar?

1  2  3  4

2 Match the correct name to each of the pictures above.

> Frankenstein's monster
> Captain Picard
> Ragetti
> Captain Hook

3 Now match each of the descriptions below to the pictures.
   a) His eye keeps popping out and rolling all over the place, only to be popped back in the eye socket again.
   b) His arm was lost to a crocodile and replaced by one that is the same as his name.
   c) This is a creature who looks like a man but who is larger than average and more powerful.
   d) He travelled into the future on the USS Enterprise and became a cyborg.

4 The examples in Exercise 3 are all fictional, but science is developing new drugs and materials where body parts can be replaced. Some of the relevant terms are given below. Match each one with its definition.

Word	Definition
Prosthetics	Cells from a donor are taken and regrown into a replacement body part in an artificial womb.
Bionic	New skin, for example, can be grown artificially this way and replace damaged skin.
Cloning	Mechanical body parts that are functional replacements and are mass-produced because they are the most economical type.
Cyborg	A human that has mechanical parts built into the body.
Regrowth	Mechanical body parts that are individually designed replacements which function better than the original.
Replicating cells	The body is stimulated to regrow its missing parts, as with bones.

5 With your partner, think about how science has helped the human body to overcome how fragile and complex it is. Make a list of some of the scientific and technological advances that have been made up to the present day and say how they are used and how they improve the body. For example:
  • Vitamin pills – to improve a person's strength and resistance to everyday diseases like the common cold.

6 How could you define and show the difference between science and technology? Complete the paragraph below with the words in the box, which will then give you a definition.

> accurate   laws   seeks   understand   questions   meet   both

Scientific inquiry is driven by the desire to _____ the natural world and _____ to answer _____ that are always uncertain and changing. Technology is driven by the need to _____ human needs and solve human problems.

_____ science and technology depend on _____ scientific information, and they cannot break scientific _____.

7 Look at the following statistics, then look at the questions and discuss them with your partner.

- By the year 2050 the number of people who will live to 100 years old will increase from 135 000 to 2.2 million.
- By 2010 biomonitoring devices will provide wearers with up-to-the-minute data about their health status.
- Implanted microchips could transmit messages to a computer that controls, for example, the heating and light systems of intelligent buildings.
  - a) If you could increase your physical strength or senses, what would you change and why?
  - b) How would society be different if most people lived until they were 100 years old?
  - c) Which of the techniques in Exercise 4 would you say were most likely to be adopted in the future? Why?
  - d) How much do you agree with the body being changed through science? Why/why not?

B Let's read 1

1 Here is some information about famous scientists and their achievements.

- Galileo – spread the idea that the Sun was the centre of the solar system rather than our planet Earth, as was originally believed.
- Charles Darwin – was criticised for his theory about evolution and the origins of man.
- Harry Griffin – involved with the cloning of Dolly the sheep.
- Patrick Steptoe – involved with the first test tube baby (where the baby was first formed outside the body of the mother).

Consider the following about the people and their achievements above:

a) How would our life be different today if the people above hadn't achieved what they did?

b) To what extent do you think they are wrong in what they did?

c) To what extent do you think they are right in what they did?

d) To what extent do you think humans will want to continue being involved in the creation or improvement of life?

e) Give examples of where you think there might be other scientific and technological advances in the future.

The book *Frankenstein* was written in 1817 by a woman called Mary Shelley and is a famous horror story about a scientist creating life.

2 Make complete sentences by matching the sentence beginnings in the box with the endings below. By doing this you will then have an outline of the story of *Frankenstein*.

The scientist is afraid of what …	He eventually finds his creator …
The creature finds his creator dead and laments …	He intends to create …
	The creature becomes bitter …
The creature is never accepted by people …	The creature escapes and …
	But the scientist is afraid of creating …
An inventive scientist …	
The scientist eventually …	He intended his human to be …

a) _____ starts meddling with dead human body parts.
b) _____ a life in the form of a human.
c) _____ beautiful but it is a monster.
d) _____ he has created and runs away.
e) _____ goes out into the world looking for friendship.
f) _____ because of its appearance.
g) _____ and cruel and commits murders.
h) _____ who he asks to create a mate for him.
i) _____ something just as evil as the first one.
j) _____ dies of exhaustion.
k) _____ and disappears off into the distance.

3 Match the words to their synonyms.

dreary	convulsive	deprived
passion	pitiable person	dull
describe	delineate	instil
toils	crossing	ardour
attempted	wretch	bursting
infuse	work	traversing
denied	endeavoured	

4 You are now going to read an extract from the story of *Frankenstein* where the scientist has just finished his creation. Find the words from the box opposite in the extract.

It was on a dreary night of November that I beheld the accomplishment of my toils. With an anxiety that almost amounted to agony, I collected the instruments of life around me, that I might infuse a spark of being into the lifeless thing that lay at my feet. It was already one in the morning; the rain pattered dismally against the panes, and my candle was nearly burnt out, when, by the glimmer of the half-extinguished light, I saw the dull yellow eye of the creature open; it breathed hard, and a convulsive motion agitated its limbs.

How can I describe my emotions at this catastrophe, or how delineate the wretch whom with such infinite pains and care I had endeavoured to form? His limbs were in proportion, and I had selected his features as beautiful. Beautiful! Great God! His yellow skin scarcely covered the work of muscles and arteries beneath; his hair was of a lustrous black, and flowing; his teeth of pearly whiteness; but these luxuriances only formed a more horrid contrast with his watery eyes, that seemed almost of the same colour as the dun-white sockets in which they were set, his shrivelled complexion and straight black lips.

The different accidents of life are not so changeable as the feelings of human nature. I had worked hard for nearly two years, for the sole purpose of infusing life into an inanimate body. For this I had deprived myself of rest and health. I had desired it with an ardour that far exceeded moderation; but now that I had finished, the beauty of the dream vanished, and breathless horror and disgust filled my heart. Unable to endure the aspect of the being I had created, I rushed out of the room and continued a long time traversing my bedchamber, unable to compose my mind to sleep.

5 Copy and complete the sentences about the extract above.
   a) The writer gives a negative feeling to the story by using words and expressions like _____.
   b) The use of these words helps give the story _____.
   c) We know that the story is not set in the modern day because _____.
   d) We know that the writer does not 'like' his creation by the use of words _____.
   e) The word that tells us that the scientist sees his creation as a disaster is _____.
   f) Find five descriptions that are given to talk about the appearance of the creature.

g) We know the creature is not beautiful because _____ .

h) We know the scientist worked for _____ to complete his creation.

i) At the end of the time the scientist felt _____ because _____ .

j) We know the scientist could not bear to look at his creation because _____ .

C Let's speak and listen

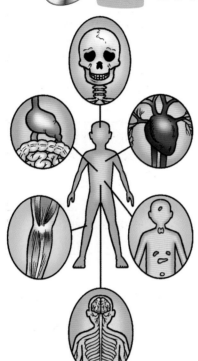

1 Look at the human body and its different systems. With your partner, first talk about what the different areas of the body are that are shown in the diagram.

Match the title of the system shown to the correct part of the body.

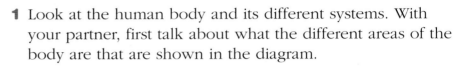

Nervous system	Digestive system	Endocrine system
Cardiovascular system	Skeletal system	Muscular system

2 Match the purpose of each of the systems.

Systems	Purpose
Cardiovascular	Where hormones are produced to help assist in normal bodily functions like growth.
Muscular	The rigid framework of the body that also protects many internal organs.
Digestive	The system responsible for carrying oxygen from the air to the blood stream.
Skeletal	Attached to the skeletal system to allow us to make certain moves.
Endocrine	Involved with the breakdown of food in the body.
Nervous	The body's information gatherer, storage centre and control system.

3 Now match each of the following parts of the body to their function in the grid below. The first one has been done for you.

pituitary gland	liver	spine	cardiac muscle
stomach	rib cage	~~heart~~	brain
sciatic nerve	pancreas	spinal cord	lungs
skull	triceps	small intestine	
thyroid	trachea	tendon	

Pumping organ of the body – *heart*	Connects the muscles to the bone	Stores and breaks down food	Releases hormones that affect growth
Bony section of the head that protects the brain	Controls the rate at which the body produces energy	Bones that protect the heart, lungs, etc.	Helps with the straightening of the arm
Supports the trunk of the body and head and protects the spinal cord	Two-way communication system between itself and arms, legs, etc.	Secretes body juices that break down fat, etc.	Breathing organs that process oxygen from the air
Where most food digestion takes place	Found in the walls of the heart	Centre of the nervous system	Cleans the blood
Largest and longest nerve in the body	Windpipe that enters the lungs		

4 Match each part of the body to its system. Use a table like the one below. There are three words for each system.

System	Part 1	Part 2	Part 3
Cardiovascular	heart		
Muscular			
Digestive			
Skeletal			
Endocrine			
Nervous			

5 Now listen to see how much of the information you got correct.

D Let's read 2

1 Do you know this story? Work out what the title is and put the pictures into the correct order.

eth yulg ncidkgul

2 Now look at these pictures and talk about what each one represents.

We can see from the story and the pictures that what is 'acceptable beauty' depends on many things, such as a person's culture, time in history, society, etc.

Science and technology have had a huge impact on this with the introduction of cosmetic surgery. Here are some terms used in cosmetic surgery:

- Liposuction – a surgical procedure that removes fatty tissue from areas of the body like the abdomen, legs, etc.
- Rhinoplasty (nose job) – a surgical procedure that alters the size or shape of the nose.
- Rhytidectomy (facelift) – surgical removal of wrinkles.

3 Bearing in mind the information and pictures in Exercise 2, talk about the following with your partner:
- What are the advantages of cosmetic surgery?
- What are the disadvantages of cosmetic surgery?
- Why is cosmetic surgery more popular in some countries than others?
- What do you think having cosmetic surgery says about a person?
- Would you ever consider having cosmetic surgery? Why/why not?
- Do you personally know anybody who has had cosmetic surgery?
- Why do more women than men have cosmetic surgery?
- Describe what would be considered socially unacceptable in your society about changing a person's appearance.

4 You are going to read a passage about women and their feet. But before you do that, say if the following sentences are true or false. Look at the feet of the Chinese women in Exercise 2 to help you.
- It used to be fashionable for women in China to have small feet.
- It was a practice that started over 1500 years ago.
- The women used to break their toes and bind them under the foot.
- Small feet mean that a woman is more beautiful.
- This was also practised in some European countries.
- Small feet guaranteed marriage and wealth for these women.
- These women could walk and work comfortably on their bound feet.
- It is now an illegal practice to bind your feet.

5 Read the title of this story. How does it refer to the tradition of Chinese foot binding?

Shoes don't fit? Try a toe tuck

British women are hot on the heels of their American counterparts when it comes to designing their feet to match their fashions, as slimming down the ankle is just one of many procedures that are becoming more popular in the UK.

Surgeons have seen a 9 per cent increase in patients requesting liposuction in the past year, a rise due in part to the thousands of women now opting to have fat sucked out of the ankle.

Slimming down the ankle is just one of many procedures that are becoming more popular in the UK, which has seen an average 54 per cent year-on-year increase in the cosmetic surgery market since 2005.

Most procedures are imports from the US, where there is a much bigger market for cosmetic podiatry. "We do whatever patients ask for – toe straightening, toe shortening, toe lengthening," said a surgeon from a New York clinic. Many of the patients at the clinic are women, who make up 99 per cent and are happy to pay from $1500 to have a single toe shortened to $15 000 to have both feet transformed into picture-perfect tootsies – paid for by cheque, by cash, by anything.

Ironically, many of the women who opt for this painful and expensive surgery are doing so because they have damaged their feet wearing high heels or shoes with pointed toes. But for many women the relationship between having beautiful feet and beautiful shoes is inseparable, whatever the cost.

Focus on grammar

Nouns and prepositions

As we saw in Unit 16, certain prepositions only go with certain verbs and the same also applies to certain nouns. The preposition can go either before or after the noun.

6 Match the correct preposition with the noun.

Prepositions before the noun				
Preposition	**Noun**			
by – for – in – on	love cheque	a walk	accident	holiday
	mistake the telephone	a swim	my opinion	lunch

Prepositions after the noun					
noun					**Preposition**
reason	break	demand	decrease	difference	with – between – for
relationship	rise	damage	photograph	connection	– in – of – to
connection	contract	cause	solution	relationship	
problem	invitation	increase			

7 Find eight examples of 'noun – preposition' or 'preposition – noun' in the passage opposite.

8 Choose one of the combinations from the tables to complete the following sentences.

a) Police have found a _____ _____ the suspect.

b) You should go _____ _____ after dinner to help you digest your food.

c) There is a big _____ _____ watching a sport and playing it.

d) She has been _____ _____ now for an hour.

e) Going on a diet is not a _____ _____ losing weight; you should do exercise as well.

f) There has been an _____ _____ the number of people having cosmetic surgery.

g) Thing is, there is the _____ _____ that long journey every time we visit them.

h) _____ _____ it is better if you try something out first before paying a lot of money for it.

i) Can I pay _____ _____ as I don't have enough cash on me?

j) There isn't much _____ _____ CDs any more as people download music.

k) There is no _____ _____ Manchester United and Manchester City except the name of the city.

l) They have sent an _____ _____ everybody in the immediate family for the wedding.

Focus on vocabulary

Headlines

Headlines in English are often difficult to understand. Look at the headline from the last passage:

Shoes don't fit? Try a toe tuck

If we look at it more closely we understand that the second part could refer to two things:

a) A toe tuck = where Chinese women used to break their toes and bind them under the foot (so tucking them under their feet).

b) The verb 'to tuck' is used in cosmetic surgery, e.g. 'a tummy tuck' where folds of the stomach are removed.

Headlines can have the following distinctive features:
- They are often incomplete sentences.
- They use abbreviations.
- They use the simple tenses.
- They use the infinitive.
- They drop auxiliary verbs and articles.

9 Look at the following headlines with your partner and together talk about the different meanings each one might have.

County officials to talk rubbish

Prison for drowning child

Giant waves on beach

Milk drinkers are turning to powder

Florida illegal aliens cut in half by new law

Soldier flies back to front

E   Let's write

1 Look at the information about the increase in cosmetic surgery given in the bar chart opposite. You are going to write a newspaper article about it, including an effective headline. Look at your notes in Unit 9 about writing for a newspaper and use the information above about headlines. Write about 250 words.

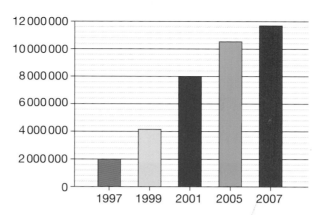

Cosmetic surgery (Surgical and Non-surgical Cosmetic Procedures: Totals)

Source: American Society for Aesthetic Plastic Surgery

F Let's do some research

You are going to find out about the latest research done in science to improve a person's life. In your research you are going to concentrate on only one area of research and an area that you think is important.

In your work, do the following:
- Explain why you have chosen that area of research and how it is important to you.
- Explain exactly what the research is and how it is going to benefit people.
- Talk about the main people who are involved in the research.
- Talk about the kind of people who will benefit from the research.
- Talk about which part of the world will benefit most from the research.
- Talk about who is doing and financing the research.
- Talk about how accessible it will be to all people.

G Let's learn something new

- There are 206 bones in the human body.
- The human eye blinks an average of 4 200 000 times a year.
- It takes approximately 12 hours for food to entirely digest.

Unit 18 The Big Bang

 Let's start

1 What is this a picture of?

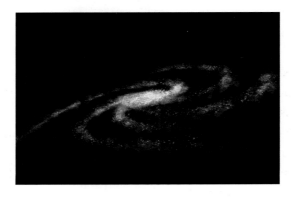

With your partner, talk about the photo and the various things that you can see.

2 Now look at the following words and talk about what each one is.

the Milky Way	satellite – mechanical	an astronomer
our solar system	a moon	an aurora
an astronaut	a planet	an astrologer
a galaxy	a star	the North Star
a telescope	the Sun	the Universe

3 What was the Big Bang? When did it happen? How did it happen?

Look at these pictures and use them to help you put the following information into the correct chronological order.

1

2

3
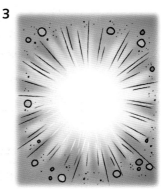

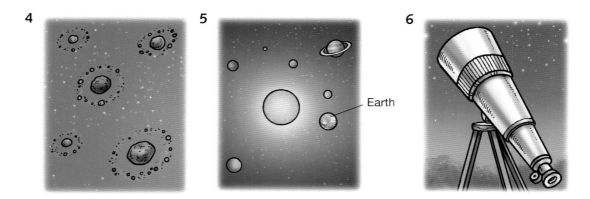

a) It exploded in a sudden burst of energy.

b) About eight or nine billion years later our solar system was formed.

c) The explosion created a small and extremely hot universe that began to expand in all directions.

d) About 15 billion years ago the universe was squeezed into a much smaller space.

e) Edwin Hubble developed the telescope that allowed for theories about the Universe to be made.

f) Over time things cooled and tiny bits of matter clumped together to form stars and galaxies.

B Let's read 1

1 With your partner, look at the table below and talk about how you think things will be different or may have changed in the future in the following areas. Add an area of your choice to the list.

	The year 2010	The year 2080	The year 2160	The year 4000	Billions of years from now
Yourself					
Advances in medicine					
Advances in technology					
Advances in science					
Society					
The Universe					
Your choice of subject					

2 Now look at the following predictions, which are based on the work of scientists and experts. How much do they agree or disagree with your ideas? How much do you think the predictions are likely to happen? Discuss them with your partner.

2010 Education Minister defends plans to electronically tag absentee school children.

An international airline this week took delivery of Goliath, a revolutionary 1000-passenger plane.

2012 Japan's right to mine the Moon for helium-3 – the most valuable substance known to Man – is being challenged.

2013 The sprinter Dave Wilson has been stripped of his Olympic gold medals following reports that he has been using nano-robots.

2042 Cities have gone as high and as wide as they can, now the challenge is to dig deep.

2043 Astronomers searching for extra-terrestrial intelligence announced today that a signal has been received.

2044 A computer worn in the ear allows people to hear a simultaneous translation regardless of the language being spoken.

2049 Three men who 'died' 30 years ago were this morning having breakfast.

Billions of years from now Our galaxy, the Milky Way, will collide with the Andromeda galaxy, resulting in the end of life as we know it.

3 With your partner, comment on the following and note your answers.

Situation	You	Your partner
More money should be spent on space research.		
Less money should be spent on space research and more spent on the world's problems.		
We will destroy our planet and make it unlivable in the future.		
Mankind will need to find other planets that can support life.		
It is impossible now to think and plan for hundreds of years into the future as we can't predict what will happen.		
Robots should be sent into space, not animals or humans.		

4 You are going to read about NASA. But what is NASA? Match the questions to the answers to find out.

Questions	Answers
What does NASA stand for?	NASA's Apollo 1 was destroyed by fire along with its crew – the astronauts had been selected for the first manned mission.
What is NASA?	It is an agency of the United States' government that is responsible for the country's space programme.
How old is NASA?	To return man to the Moon in 2018 and for spacecraft to visit all the planets of the solar system.
What was one of NASA's greatest achievements?	In 2008 its budget was $17.3 billion.
What is the motto of NASA?	The National Aeronautics & Space Administration.
About how much is spent by NASA?	The first walk on the Moon by man in 1969.
What happened in 1967?	It celebrated its 50th birthday in 2008.
What are NASA's future plans?	For the benefit of all.

5 Now read the following passage quickly and count how many times you read the word NASA.

A call for Moon and Mars colonies

A scientist from the UK's University of Cambridge called for massive investment in establishing colonies on the Moon and Mars. He argued that the world should devote about 10 times as much as NASA's current budget – or 0.25% of the world's financial resources – to space.

He has previously spoken in favour of colonising space as an insurance policy against the possibility of humanity being wiped out by catastrophes like nuclear war and climate change. He argues that humanity should eventually expand to other solar systems.

He delivered a speech at NASA's 50th anniversary where he focused on near-term possibilities, backing the goals of returning astronauts to the Moon by 2020 and sending humans to Mars soon after that. This, according to a NASA study, could be achieved by the early 2030s. He said, "Robotic missions are much cheaper and may provide more scientific information, but they don't catch the public imagination in the same way, and they don't spread the human race into space. If the human race is to continue for another million years, we will have to boldly go where no one has gone before." He added that, "Humanity should try to expand to Earth-like planets around other stars and although we can't envision them with the current technology, we should make interstellar travel a long-term aim and by long-term I mean over the next 200 to 500 years." He then went on to say that, "Humanity can afford to battle earthly problems like climate change and still have plenty of resources left over for colonising space."

The scientist also speculated on the reasons that SETI (Search for Extra-Terrestrial Intelligence) projects have not yet detected any alien civilisations. He offered three possibilities: that life of any kind is very rare in the universe; that simple life forms are common, but intelligent life rare; or that intelligent life tends to quickly destroy itself. "Personally, I prefer the second possibility – that primitive life is relatively common, but that intelligent life is very rare," he said. "Some would say it has yet to occur on Earth."

6 Now answer these questions.
- **a)** What figure in dollars was suggested should be spent on NASA? (See Exercise 4.)
- **b)** Is this the first time that the scientist has talked about this issue?
- **c)** What word in the text shows that he supports NASA's plans to go to the Moon in 2020?
- **d)** Does he think NASA's plans for landing humans on Mars are happening soon enough? How do we know that?
- **e)** In your own words, explain why he does not support robots going on space missions.
- **f)** What advantages do robots have over humans in space missions?
- **g)** Where does he suggest that humans have no long-term future on Earth?
- **h)** Does he suggest that space research should be given priority over earthly problems?
- **i)** What is meant by the words 'Some would say that it has yet to occur on Earth'?
- **j)** Which reason would you support for no evidence of extra-terrestrial life? Give your reason.

C # Let's speak and listen

1 With your partner, look at this quiz and see how many of the questions you can answer.

	Space quiz
1	What was the name of the spaceship that went to the Moon in 1969?
2	What language does the word 'Galaxy' come from?
3	How many stars are there in the Milky Way?
4	How far is the Sun from the Earth?
5	What is the temperature of the Sun?
6	What are asteroids?
7	Which planet is the hottest?
8	Which planet is the largest?
9	Which planet is the furthest from the Sun?
10	Which planet is the closest to the Sun?
11	Which planet has the most moons?
12	Which planet is the brightest object in the night sky?
13	Who was the first astronaut to walk on the Moon?
14	Which country had the first space station?
15	Which was the first planet to be seen by a telescope?
16	What is the Sun made out of?
17	What planet comes after Venus in distance from the Sun?
18	Which two planets have no moons?
19	How long does light from the Sun take to reach Earth?
20	When was the first part of the International Space Station launched?

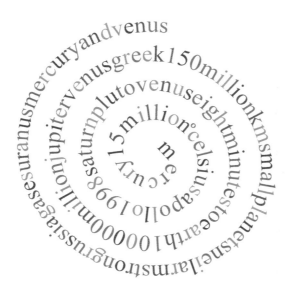

2 The answers are all mixed up in this word circle. First separate the words and then match them to the answers. Put capital letters where necessary.

3 Now listen and check that your answers are correct.

D Let's read 2

In the passage on pages 227–228, we read that the scientist believed that intelligent life is rare and this is why none has been discovered yet. People have always been fascinated about extra-terrestrial life and messages have often been sent into space to try to communicate with any intelligent forms there.

An example is this message sent out by a radio dish.

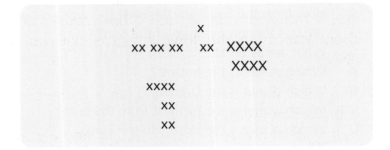

1 What do you understand from this message? What is it trying to tell you? Would you understand it if you were an intelligent alien?

Identify the following features from the message:
   a) The Sun.
   b) The nine planets.
   c) Earth highlighted and separated from the rest of the planets to show its significance.
   d) An indication of the planets' size.

2 Look at the pictures below and, with your partner, discuss whether they reflect how you imagine life from another planet to be.

Would your idea be different? Describe it to your partner.

3 An alien's appearance might show where it comes from. Think about how human beings' bodies are indicative of the planet we come from. Think of at least five different features with your partner, for example:

We have lungs that breathe in air: the oxygen is used in the body but the carbon dioxide is expelled.

4 One of the planets in our solar system that has always interested people is Mars. What do you think life forms from Mars would be like? Why? What do you know about Mars? With your partner, talk about Mars and write down any facts that you know about the planet.

5 Now look at the information about Mars below – can you complete any of the gaps?

- It is also known as the _____ and the _____.
- It can get very cold with temperatures at _____.
- Like Earth it has _____ at the north and south.
- It is rich in _____ which gives it its red colour.

  - It has the highest _____ in the solar system.
  - There is evidence that _____ used to flow there.
  - It has two moons called _____.
  - It takes about _____ to go round the Sun.
  - It would take about _____ to travel to Mars.
  - It is about _____ the size of Earth.
  - It has a thin _____ atmosphere, which is not breathable.
  - Its conditions are the _____ to those on Earth compared with any other planet in the solar system.

6 Look at the words in the box below and put the correct words into the appropriate gaps in the sentences above.

Phobos and Deimos	Roman God of War	most similar
5.25 Earth months	−140°C	686.98 Earth days
volcano	poles	half
carbon dioxide	iron	
Red Planet	water	

7 You are now going to read an extract from a book called *Out of the Silent Planet* where a man is taken to a planet called Malacandra, which is in fact Mars.

Make a note of the information you already have about the appearance of Mars and note the differences with the description of Malacandra. How are they different?

On one side the water extended a long way and seemed to be flowing over a shallow, broken and swirling water that made a softer and more hissing sound than water on earth; and where it washed the bank — the pinkish-white vegetation went down to the very edge. Then in the distance he could see a mass of something purple, so huge that he took it for a heather-covered mountain. Beyond these were strange upright shapes of whitish green; too jagged and irregular for buildings, too thin and steep for mountains. Beyond and above these again was the rose-coloured cloud-like mass. It might really be a cloud but it was very solid-looking and did not seem to have moved since he first set eyes on it. It looked like the top of a gigantic red cauliflower — or like a huge bowl of red soapsuds — and it was exquisitely beautiful in tint and shape.

Baffled by this, he turned his attention to the nearer shore beyond the shallows and suddenly his eyes mastered the object. The purple stuff was vegetation. He looked again more carefully and saw that more precisely it was vegetables, vegetables about twice the size of large trees, but apparently soft and flimsy.

Focus on grammar

Sentences

There are three main sentence types: simple, compound and complex. Knowing how and when to use each type is important because varying their use makes your writing more interesting and natural.

8 Match the three types of sentences in the table that follows with an example from the extract above and its purpose.

Sentence type	Example	Purpose
Simple sentence	Then in the distance he could see a mass of something purple, so huge that he took it for a heather-covered mountain.	They join two or more independent clauses which are of equal importance.
Compound sentence	The purple stuff was vegetation.	These join one or more <u>dependent</u> clauses to the independent clause.
Complex sentence	It might really be a cloud but it was very solid-looking and did not seem to have moved since he first set eyes on it.	Contains only one independent clause.

9 Look at the following sentences and identify whether they are simple, compound or complex.
   a) Some students like to study at night-time.
   b) My father went to watch the football, so my mother went shopping.
   c) When he handed in his test, he remembered that he had not done the last page.
   d) Peter and Jane went to the cinema, after they had finished their homework.
   e) Alma likes to study at the library every day.
   f) I ate a bowl of fruit but then I didn't want to eat my dinner.

A thing to be careful about in English is the use of commas. Commas should not be used to join two whole sentences together.

10 All the following sentences have the comma used incorrectly. Rewrite them using a joining word rather than a comma. For example:

   The milk had finished, he went to get some more.
   The milk had finished **so** he went to get some more.

   a) The cats kept crying, they had not eaten since morning.
   b) The woman stopped crying, she was still very sad.
   c) The long dry summer passed, still no sign of rain.
   d) My first lesson seemed to go really well, I was feeling really nervous.
   e) Do you want to use the computer, shall I switch it off?
   f) He walked out of the seminar, the speaker hadn't finished.

11 Look at the examples below the most important joining words. In your writing, attempt to use different types to make your writing more interesting.

and	although	as	because	but	if
or	before	after	until	since	when
whenever	while	though	whether	where	

Complete the sentences using a different joining word for each one.
a) He listens to music _____ he does his homework.
b) They bought milk _____ bread.
c) They didn't go out for a walk _____ it was raining.
d) Remember that place _____ you fell down the stairs?
e) They were allowed to go out only _____ they had done their jobs.
f) She hoses down the verandah _____ it rains.
g) He doesn't like classical music _____ listens to it sometimes.
h) He gave the dog some water _____ he saw that its bowl was empty.
i) He doesn't like going shopping _____ he would never tell you.
j) I will come with you _____ you pay for my ticket.
k) They are not allowed out _____ they have cleaned their rooms.
l) He likes to play football _____ does his brother.
m) He could speak very good French _____ he had never been to France.
n) He came _____ the bell rang so he was early.
o) It was a great match _____ you saw it live or on TV.
p) You can come now _____ later – choose.
q) School hasn't been the same _____ I changed class.

Focus on vocabulary

Descriptive words

In the passage on page 232 the writer used some very descriptive words to describe the scene he could see. Some examples are:

- 'pinkish-white' – used to describe colour.
- 'jagged and irregular' – used to describe shape.

12 Find two more examples of descriptive words or expressions from the passage and say what it is they are describing.

13 Look at the following descriptive words and put each one into the category that it would be used to describe. There are four words to fit in each of the categories. One has been done already. You may need to use a dictionary to help you.

~~protruding~~	decent	deceitful	musty	streamlined
transparent	talented	tactful	unrefined	prejudiced
swishing	virtuous	dainty	graceless	intolerant
profound	courteous	tinkling	clattering	sweaty
insolent	clumsy	twinkling	irrational	emerald
curly	soothing	shallow	moist	objective
rotten	scratchy	notorious	fluffy	agile
polished	drooping	ruby	perfumed	intellectual

Sound	Touch	Colour and visual	Smell	Pattern and shape
				protruding – n
A written text	**Physical qualities**	**Mental qualities**	**Moral qualities**	**Social qualities**

14 Now decide if the words have a positive (p) or negative (n) meaning.

E Let's write

Paragraphs

1 Say if the following sentences about paragraphs are true or false.
   a) A new paragraph should be started when you write about a new idea.
   b) When a new character speaks you should start a new paragraph.
   c) The first paragraph is indented (meaning to set the first line of a paragraph in from the margin).
   d) Paragraphs following the first paragraph are indented.
   e) Block paragraphing is where a line is left between paragraphs.
   f) Block paragraphing is used for informal letters.
   g) In block paragraphing indents are also used.
   h) A paragraph can have one or many sentences.

2 Look back at the passage 'A call for Moon and Mars colonies' (pages 227–228) and answer the following questions about its paragraphing.

a) How is the first paragraph started? Why?

b) How is the second paragraph started? Why?

c) What is the main focus of the first paragraph?

d) Why does the writer start the second paragraph with the words 'He has previously spoken in favour …'?

e) How many paragraphs are there in the whole passage?

f) What is the focus of each of the paragraphs?

g) Give each of the paragraphs a title.

3 You are now going to write three paragraphs on one of the following topics. Each of your paragraphs should have at least four sentences and should include simple, compound and complex sentences as well as vocabulary taken from Section D Exercise 13.

- The day the Earth stood still
- Visions of Venus
- The Big Bang

F Let's do some research

You are going to research the Big Bang and find the answers to the following questions.

a) What is CERN and what connection is there with the Big Bang?

b) Who was Georges Lamaître?

c) What did Edwin Hubble discover in 1929?

d) Who is Fred Hoyle and what did he do?

e) What discovery did the Astro-2 observatory make?

G Let's learn something new

- Because of lower gravity, a person who weighs 100 kg on earth would only weigh 38 kg on the surface of Mars.
- In 2006, astronomers changed the definition of a planet. This means that Pluto is now referred to as a dwarf planet.
- Footprints and tyre tracks left behind by astronauts on the moon will stay there forever as there is no wind to blow them away.